Home
Sewn
Home

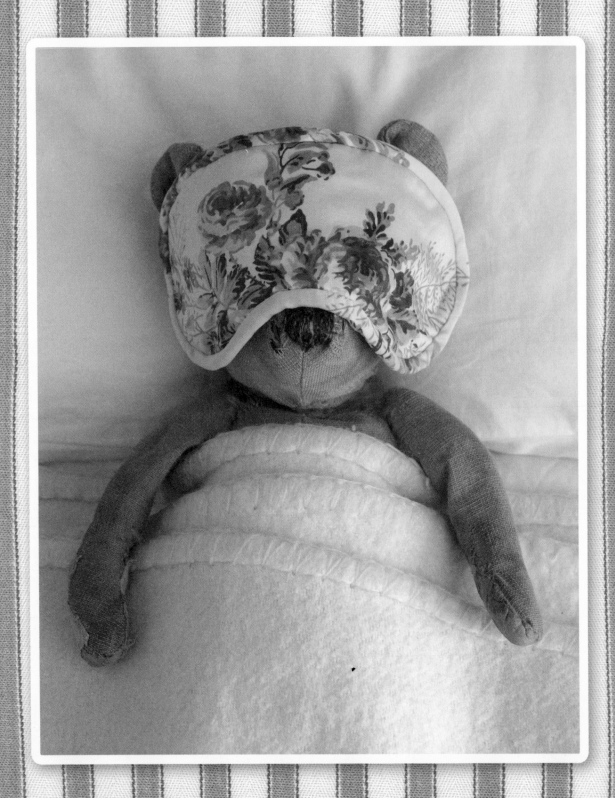

Sally Walton

Home Sewn Home

20 Projects to Make

for the Retro Home

To my daughter Roxy, who makes me happy and also loves to sew.

First published 2012 by
Guild of Master Craftsman Publications Ltd
Castle Place, 166 High Street, Lewes,
East Sussex BN7 1XU

Text © Sally Walton, 2012
Copyright in the Work © GMC Publications Ltd, 2012

ISBN 978 1 86108 840 6

A catalogue record for this book is available
from the British Library.

Publisher: Jonathan Bailey
Production Manager: Jim Bulley
Managing Editor: Gerrie Purcell
Senior Project Editor: Dominique Page
Editor: Sarah Hoggett
Managing Art Editor: Gilda Pacitti
Photographer: Tim Clinch

Colour origination by GMC Reprographics
Printed and bound by 1010 Printing Ltd

Contents

Introduction 8

Gallery 10

LIVING ROOM

Envelope Cushion 32

Doorstop 36

Screen Cover 40

Storage Box 44

KITCHEN & UTILITY

Oven Gloves 50

Ironing Board Cover 54

Coffee Cozy.........................58

Peg Bag...............................62

Pretty Girly Apron 66

Butcher's Apron 70

Plastic Bag Keeper...............74

BEDROOM

Nightdress or Pyjama Case ..80

Travel Shoebag 84

Padded Coat Hanger............88

Eye Mask.............................92

Jewellery Roll 96

BATHROOM

Wash Bag............................102

Laundry Bag 106

Bath Cap 110

Hairstyling Bag..................114

SUPPLIES & TECHNIQUES

Retro-style & Recycled Fabrics 120

Basic Sewing Kit 122

Working with Patterns 126

Machine Sewing.................128

Pinning, Tacking & Hemming.....................130

Finishing Seams 133

Gathering...........................136

Fastenings 138

Embroidery Stitches 143

Eyelets 146

Trimmings.........................147

Sewing Terms....................152

Blogs 154

Suppliers 155

Acknowledgements............157

Index 158

Introduction

There is something magical about sewing, particularly when it makes three dimensions out of two. If it were quicker, people would pay good money to see a flat piece of cloth turn into a free-standing bag, but most of the time it remains a private pleasure, albeit one that can last a lifetime.

A couple of generations back, all girls had sewing lessons in school while boys did carpentry. It would be a lie to suggest that everyone loved it, but even those who didn't at least learnt the basics. Then the subjects began to disappear from the curriculum, only to be studied as a career choice. Suddenly life was all about speed, technology and purchasing items. Sewing machine sales dropped to an all-time low and handmade was not a style to aspire to.

Who knew that this trend would reverse so soon? Now the sewing supplies industry is booming and 'Learn to Sew' classes are springing up in cool urban districts everywhere. Let's face it: in the second decade of the 21st century, sewing is hot!

The aim of this book is to encourage you to make things yourself, for the lasting pleasure and satisfaction that it brings. If you are new to sewing, start with one of the easy projects such as the cushion cover on page 32. Take your time to get it right, then sit back and admire your achievement. Even if your first attempt is a bit wonky, that's all part of the fun!

p.32

p.36

p.40

p.44

p.50

p.54

p.58

p.62

p.66

p.70

p.74

p.80

p.84

p.88

☞ p.92

p.96

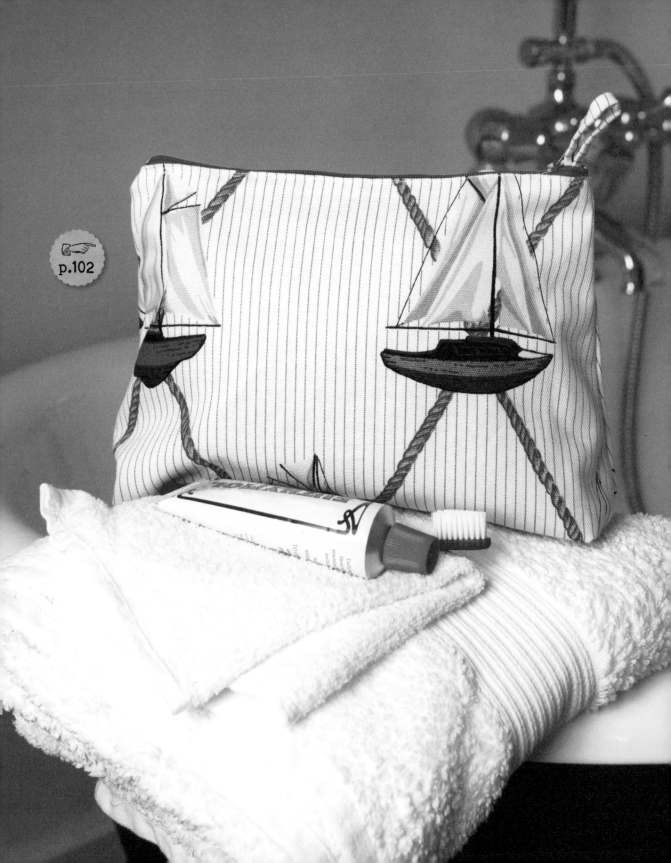

p.102

p.106

p.110

p.114

Living Room

Envelope Cushion

A new cushion can give any room an instant, fresh look, and this envelope style is very quick and easy to make. If vintage is your thing, search around for an old curtain like the one used here, which dates back to the 1950s. If you prefer a more contemporary look, have a rummage through the fabric remnants in your local interiors store.

CUTTING LIST:

CUSHION FRONT
19 × 19in (48.5 × 48.5cm)
Cut one in feature fabric

CUSHION BACK
19 × 13in (48.5 × 33cm)
Cut two in feature fabric

SUPPLIES:

1yd (1m) feature fabric, plus ½yd (50cm) extra for piping

2yd 6in (2m) medium-width covered piping cord

18in (46cm) feather or polyester cushion pad

Basic sewing kit (see page 122)

Instructions:

1 Draw a diagonal line between two corners of the ½yd (50cm) of fabric for the piping. Mark out diagonal lines 2in (5cm) apart and cut the fabric into strips. Make the piping, following the instructions on page 150.

2 Place the fabric for the cushion front right side up. Pin the piping around the edge, with the cord on the inside and the raw edge aligned with the edge of the fabric. Snip the fabric up to the cord at the corners.

3 Where the two ends of the piping meet, open the piped seam and snip away the cord to allow the two ends to overlap smoothly. Now angle the ends back towards the edge.

4 Fit a zipper foot to the machine and sew the piping in place, keeping as close to the cord as you can.

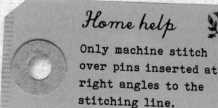

Home help

Only machine stitch over pins inserted at right angles to the stitching line.

5 Fold one long edge of each back piece under by 1in (2.5cm). Pin and press. Remove the pins, then fold the raw edge under to meet the press mark. Pin, press and machine stitch close to the folded edge.

6 Place the cushion front right side up. Place the two back pieces on top, right sides down, with the raw edges aligning and the hemmed edges overlapping each other in the centre. Pin the outside seam on the outside of the 'bump' of the cord. Sew slowly, using a zipper foot pressed up close to the cord. Trim the seam allowances and cut off the corners close to the stitching line.

7 Turn the cushion cover right side out and press. Insert the cushion pad.

Doorstop

A doorstop is one of those useful things that you manage to live without until you own one – then you wonder how you coped. The cube can be filled with rice, lentils or any other small grain. You could also use sand, which is heavier, but it will need to be contained inside a plastic bag to prevent grains from escaping through the seams.

If you have quite a lightweight door and no draughts, then you won't need the doorstop to be this big; simply adjust the size of the squares to make the size you want.

CUTTING LIST:

1 CUBE SIDES
Cut six in upholstery fabric

2 HANDLE
Cut one in upholstery fabric

SUPPLIES:

Patterns 1 and 2 from pattern sheet F

½yd (50cm) upholstery fabric

11 lb (5kg) sack of rice

Plastic bag (optional)

Basic sewing kit (see page 122)

Home help

A close-weave upholstery fabric is best for this project, as it will be sturdy enough to withstand heavy wear and hold in the rice.

Instructions:

1 Fold the fabric for the handle in half lengthways, wrong sides together, and press. Tuck the long edges under by ¼in (6mm) and pin in place, then topstitch along both long sides.

2 Mark the halfway points on opposite sides of one square, then sew one of the handle ends in place along each seam line. This square will be the top of the cube.

3 With right sides together, pin another square to the top square. Using a ½-in (12-mm) seam allowance on all seams, beginning and ending ½in (12mm) from the end of each seam, stitch the two squares together along one edge.

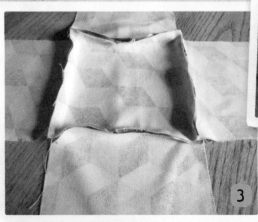

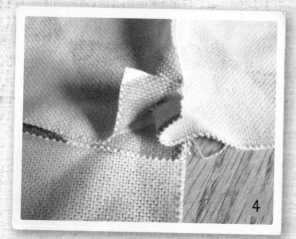

4 Continue adding squares all around the top square in this way, taking care to sew through only two layers at the corners and to keep all the seams the same width.

5 Attach the last square to three of the base edges. Sew 2in (5cm) in from each corner of the last open seam, leaving a gap for filling.

6 Now turn the doorstop the right side out by reaching inside and pulling the handle through and push all the corners out so that you have a square. Fill the cube with rice, then sew up the seam by hand using small, even stitches.

Home help

Scooping your rice up into a jug will make it easier to pour into the opening of your doorstop.

Screen Cover

Most living rooms are arranged with the television as the focal point. Here's a way to break its dominance by making a pretty cover: it's a bit like covering the parrot cage when you need a break from the constant bird chatter!

The idea works just as well for a computer screen – once it's tucked up out of sight, who knows what you might achieve with all your extra spare time?

SUPPLIES:

Fabric for the outer cover (see 'Measuring & Cutting' below for length)

Plain lining fabric (see 'Measuring & Cutting' below for length)

Basic sewing kit (see page 122)

MEASURING & CUTTING:

To work out the width of your fabric, measure horizontally across the TV or computer screen, then add 1in (2.5cm) for the seam allowance plus the depth of the screen.

To work out the height, measure vertically from bottom and across the top, then add 2in (5cm) for the hem. Double this number for the length measurement.

If you want to cover a television or computer stand, too, then include its height in your measurement and double it.

Cut one piece of outer fabric and one piece of lining fabric the same size.

Instructions:

1 Fold the outer piece in half lengthways, right sides together, and pin. Machine stitch down each side, using a ½in (12mm) seam. Repeat with the lining fabric. Press the seams open.

2 To make a gusset, flatten the side seam at the folded end and pinch the two layers of fabric together to form a triangle.

3 Machine stitch a line across the triangle at the point where it's ½in (12mm) wider than the screen depth. Repeat on the other side seam. Trim away the pointed tips of the triangles. Repeat steps 2 and 3 with the lining fabric.

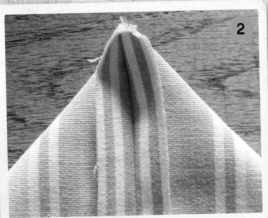

4 Turn the outer piece right side out, leaving the lining wrong side out. Now slip the lining inside the outer piece, aligning the seams.

5 Next, turn over a 1in (2.5cm) hem inside both the outer and the lining pieces and pin them together.

6 Topstitch, keeping close to the edge, then press the corners.

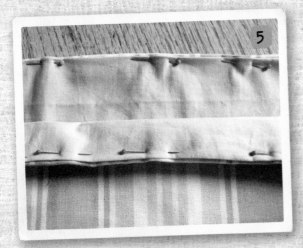

SAFETY FIRST

It is best to use smooth, natural fabrics for this project, as they are less likely to attract static electricity and cling to the screen.

Storage Box

CUTTING LIST:

3 BOX LID

Cut one in outer fabric and one in lining fabric

4 BOX SIDES

Cut one in outer fabric and one in lining fabric

BOX LID

8¹⁄₂in × 14¹⁄₂in (21.5 × 36.7cm)

Cut one in cardboard stiffener

BOX SIDES

21 × 6¹⁄₄in (53 × 16cm)

Cut two in cardboard stiffener

Home help

Choose a heavier-weight fabric with some 'body' for this project.

There are some things that we enjoy having around the home but don't like the look of – and a stack of DVDs certainly falls into this category. This soft box can store twenty of them neatly out of view.

The design shown here is based on a large shoe box and the pattern measurements could be adapted to make a cover for an existing box.

SUPPLIES:

Patterns 3 and 4 from pattern sheets A and B

1yd (1m) outer fabric

1yd (1m) lining fabric

Cardboard

Basic sewing kit (see page 122)

Craft knife and steel ruler

Cutting mat or other safe cutting surface

Home help

The lining used here is artist's canvas and the cardboard is mount board.

Instructions:

1 Draw a line 7½in (19cm) from one short end of each piece of cardboard for the box sides. Using a craft knife and steel ruler on a cutting mat, lightly score across the cardboard; this will allow the cardboard to bend crisply at the corner but not come apart.

2 Bring the edges together at the four corners of the outer fabric of the box and pin. Machine stitch, using a ½in (12mm) seam. It is important to keep all seams the same width. Do the same with the lid. Repeat to make a box and lid in the lining fabric (**2a**).

3 Turn the outer box the right side out and slip the lining inside so that the raw edges face each other, aligning the corner seams. Slip the cardboard strips between the two fabrics. Fold the raw edges of both the outer and lining fabrics over to the wrong side, allowing a clear 1in (2.5cm) of fabric above the cardboard.

4 Pin the outer and lining fabrics together around the top edge.

5 Topstitch the outer and lining fabrics together along the top edge by machine or slipstitch by hand. Machining is a bit awkward, but it's possible! Just take your time.

6 Turn the outer box lid the right side out and slip the lining inside so that the raw edges face each other, aligning the corner seams. Fold the raw edges of both the outer and lining fabric lids over to the wrong side and topstitch around one short and two long sides. Slip the cardboard into the lid, then topstitch the last side by machine or slipstitch by hand.

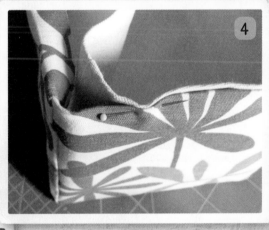

Kitchen & Utility

Oven Gloves

CUTTING LIST:

GLOVE
36 × 16in (92 × 41cm)
Cut one in feature fabric

POCKETS
18 × 16in (46 × 31cm)
Cut two in feature fabric

WADDING
7¾ × 6¾in (19 × 17cm)
Cut four in wadding

HANGING LOOP
2 × 1in (5 × 2.5cm)
Cut one in feature fabric

When a hot dish has to come out of the oven, reaching for a tea towel isn't the safest option. Instead of risking a burn, protect your hands with oven gloves made from your favourite fabric padded with a heat-resistant lining. These gloves can be made in an afternoon, to be revealed with a flourish at dinnertime.

SUPPLIES:

1yd (1m) cotton feature fabric

½yd (50cm) heat-reflecting or cotton wadding

½yd (50cm) ready-made bias binding, 1½in (4cm) wide

Basic sewing kit (see page 122)

Home help

Do not use polyester wadding for this project, as heat from the oven could cause it to melt.

Instructions:

1 Fold the fabric for the glove in half lengthways, right sides together. Using a ¼in (6mm) seam, machine stitch the ends and the side seam, leaving a 4in (10cm) gap in the middle of the seam. Turn right side out and press flat. Slip one of the wadding pieces into each end.

2 Now measure 8in (20cm) from each short end and sew a line of stitching to keep the wadding in place.

3 Fold the two pocket pieces in half lengthways, right sides together, and machine stitch the side seams, using a ¼in (6mm) seam. Turn right side out and slip a piece of wadding inside each one. Cut strips of ready-made bias binding, open out one seam and pin along the top edges of the pockets, right sides together and aligning the edges (see page 148).

4 Machine stitch the bias binding along the raw edge along the first fold line in the binding, then fold it over to the other side of the pocket and slipstitch by hand. Fold the ends in neatly as you do this.

5 Fold the fabric for the loop in half lengthways and press, tuck under the raw long edges and machine stitch along the open long edge. Fold the strip in half widthways and stitch across the two short ends to make a loop. Slip it inside the open seam at the halfway point and tack it in place.

6 Pin a pocket to each end. Lastly, machine stitch all around the outside edge to fix the pockets in place, close the seam and secure the hanging loop.

Ironing Board Cover

Ironing boards last for decades, but their covers wear out and need replacing. Even if you buy a ready-made one, you still have to fit it – but with a little more effort you can have one made from fabric that you actually enjoy looking at. And this one is reversible: when one side looks worn, flip it over for a brand new look! Household tasks seem less tedious when you surround yourself with some home-sewn style.

CUTTING LIST:

WADDING
Cut one piece the same size as your pattern (see step 1)

TOP FABRIC
Cut one piece 3in (7.5cm) larger all around than your pattern (see step 2)

BOTTOM FABRIC
Cut one piece 3in (7.5cm) larger all around than your pattern (see step 2)

SUPPLIES:

Brown parcel paper to make pattern

1½yd (1.5m) 100% cotton fabric for the top of the cover

1½ yd (1.5m) 100% cotton fabric for the bottom of the cover

1½yd (1.5m) heat-reflecting or cotton wadding

3yd (3m) ⅛in (3mm) cord

Basic sewing kit (see page 122)

Tapestry needle or safety pin for threading

Cord stopper (optional)

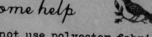

Home help

Do not use polyester fabric or wadding for this project, as they could melt under a hot iron.

Instructions:

1 To make your pattern, place the ironing board on a sheet of brown paper, then draw around the shape and cut it out. Pin the pattern to the wadding and cut out one piece.

2 Pin the pattern to the fabric for the bottom of the cover and draw around the shape, adding an extra 3in (7.5cm) all around. Cut out. Repeat with the fabric for the top of the cover. Measure 2½in (4cm) from the corner at the short flat end

in both directions. Mark, then draw a connecting line between them. Cut along the line to create a sloping corner. Repeat on the other side.

3 Centre the wadding on the bottom fabric, making sure that there is the same amount of fabric overlap on all edges. Using zig-zag stitch, stitch along the edge of the wadding to sew the two layers together.

Home help

Remove the old ironing board cover and use it as your pattern; if the wadding inside is still in good condition, it can be re-used.

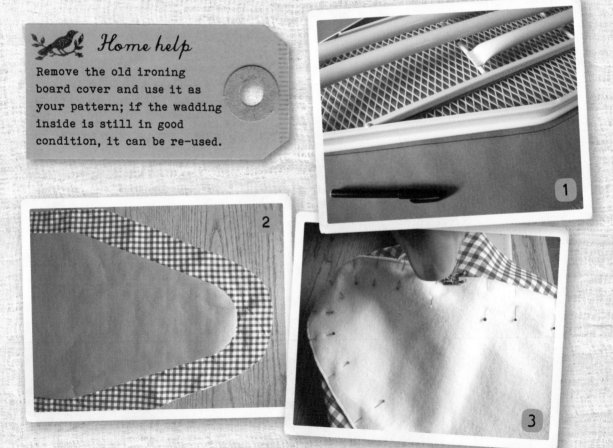

4 Place the top fabric right side up with the bottom fabric on top, wadding side uppermost. Pin the edges and sew around the outer edge, using a ¼in (6mm) seam and leaving the short straight end and one of the sloping corners open (**4a**). Then zig-zag stitch around the seam allowance to prevent fraying.

5 Turn the cover right side out. Fold over a ¼in (6mm) hem on both fabrics of the open sloping corner and machine stitch each layer

separately. Fold in the raw edges along the short straight end and topstitch both layers together close to the edge.

6 Starting at one side of an open corner and finishing at the other, sew a 1in (2.5cm) channel all the way around the cover. Thread the cord through the channel, using a tapestry needle or safety pin to guide it through. Put the cover on the board, pull up the cord and either tie the ends or use a cord stopper.

Coffee Cozy

You can't beat a cafetière or coffee press for convenience when making fresh ground coffee. But you know how it is: you've just pushed the plunger, the aroma is all around – and there's a knock on the door. When you get back the coffee's gone cold. Buy yourself some time by making this cozy jacket to keep your coffee pot hot.

Home help

If you can't get hold of heat-reflecting wadding use either cotton quilter's wadding or felt.

CUTTING LIST:

This pattern is for an average six-cup coffee press 6in (15cm) high with a 12in (30cm) circumference. Measure your coffee press and adapt the size to fit.

5 COZY
13 x 7in (33 x 17cm)
Cut one in outer fabric and one in lining fabric

6 INSULATING LAYER
12 x 6in (30 x 15cm)
Cut one in heat-reflecting wadding or felt

7 FLAP
4 x 3in (10 x 7.5cm)
Cut one in outer fabric and one in lining fabric

SUPPLIES:

Patterns 5–7 from pattern sheet C

20 x 20in (50 x 50cm) outer fabric

20 x 20in (50 x 50cm) lining fabric

12 x 6in (30 x 15cm) heat-reflecting wadding or felt

2in (5cm) hook-and-loop tape, 1in (2.5cm) wide

Basic sewing kit (see page 122)

Instructions:

1 Pin the lining and the outer fabric flap pieces right sides together. Machine stitch around one long and two short sides, about ¼in (6mm) from the edge.

2 Turn the flap right side out and press. Repeat step 1 with the lining and outer fabric pieces for the cozy.

3 Centre the wadding on top of the lining fabric and pin in place, making sure the border is the same size all the way around.

4 Machine stitch along the edge of the wadding around one short and two long sides. Turn the piece right side out and press.

5 Fold the raw edges of the open end in neatly, slotting the flap in the middle between the layers. Topstitch all the way across the open end, close to the edge.

6 Stitch one side of the hook-and-loop tape to the inside of the flap. Put the cover on the coffee press to check the fit, then pin and stitch the matching piece of hook-and-loop tape to the outside of the cozy.

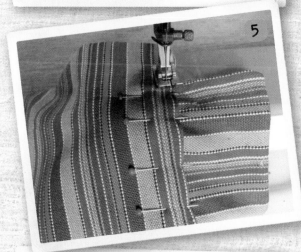

Peg Bag

There is something very comforting and homely about pegging washing out on a line to dry and the sight of a peg bag hanging on the line with the laundry reinforces the feeling. Vintage natural fabrics will fade in the sunshine and the bag will soon look like a family heirloom.

CUTTING LIST:

8 UPPER FRONT
Cut one in outer fabric and one in lining fabric

9 BACK
Cut one in outer fabric and one in lining fabric

10 LOWER FRONT
Cut one in outer fabric and one in lining fabric

HANGING LOOP
2 × 1in (5 × 2.5cm)
Cut two in outer fabric

SUPPLIES:

Child's wooden coat hanger or an adult wooden hanger plus a fine-toothed saw and sandpaper (see step 1)

Patterns 8–10 from pattern sheet A

30 × 12in (76 × 30cm) outer fabric

28 × 12in (71 × 30cm) lining fabric

1 button, 1in (2.5cm) in diameter

Basic sewing kit (see page 122)

Instructions:

1 If you are using an adult hanger cut it down to 11in (28cm) wide. Place a ruler on top and make a mark 5½in (14cm) on either side of the hook. Use a fine-toothed saw to cut away any excess and sandpaper to smooth the end.

2 Fold the fabric for the loop in half lengthways then press. Now tuck under the raw long edges and machine stitch along the open long edge, stitching as close to the edge as possible. Fold the strip in half widthways and stitch across the two short ends to make a loop.

3 Pin the lining and outer fabric upper front pieces right sides together and machine stitch around the two sides and the curved top edge. Turn right side out. Turn the raw edges under by ¼ in (6mm), positioning the loop in the centre, and pin in place. Sew the seam close to the edge and check that the hanger will fit.

4 Next, pin the lining and outer fabric lower front pieces right sides together. Machine stitch around the sides and top edge. Repeat with the lining and outer fabric back pieces. Turn both

pieces right side out and press all the seams. Turn under the raw bottom edges of both pieces, pin together, and machine stitch.

5 With wrong sides together, aligning the bottom edges, pin the lower front to the back. Machine stitch together along the sides and bottom edge of the lower front.

6 With wrong sides together, aligning the top edges, pin the upper front to the back. Machine stitch them together along the sides and top edges, leaving a ¼in (6mm) gap in the centre of the top edge for the hook of the hanger. The top piece will overlap the lower front by 1in (2.5cm). As this piece is marginally bigger there will be a raised opening.

7 Hand stitch a button onto the lower front to correspond with the loop. Contrasting thread adds a touch of individuality.

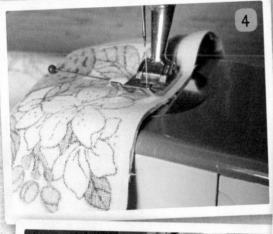

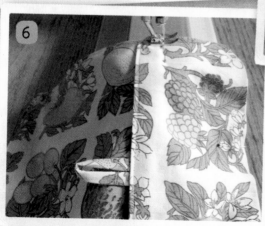

Pretty Girly Apron

CUTTING LIST:

11 POCKET
Cut one in vintage cotton fabric
and one in lining fabric

12 WAISTBAND
Cut two in vintage cotton fabric

13 SKIRT
Cut one in vintage cotton fabric

14 STRAPS
Cut two in vintage cotton fabric

A very long time ago, so the story goes, a wife would pop one of these aprons over her cocktail frock in the evening to serve canapés and drinks. That's how it looked in 1950s advertisements, anyway!

These days we are more likely to be eating around the kitchen table with friends, where one of these pretty aprons will make a cool, domestic fashion statement.

SUPPLIES:

Patterns 11–14 from pattern sheet C

1yd (1m) vintage cotton fabric

Small piece of lining fabric for the pocket

2yd (2m) rick-rack or other trimming

Basic sewing kit
(see page 122)

Instructions:

1 With right sides together, machine stitch the pocket and pocket lining pieces together along the side and bottom edges, leaving the top edge open. Turn right side out, press, then turn the top edges of both pieces in by ¼in (6mm) and pin. Pin rick-rack all around the back of the pocket, leaving half of each 'scallop' sticking out beyond the edge, and stitch in place, using matching thread. Pin and stitch another length of rick-rack across the centre front of the pocket.

2 Double hem the sides of the apron skirt (see page 131), turning over ¼in (6mm) and then ⅜in (1cm) to the wrong side. Sew two rows of gathering stitches (see page 131) along the top of the skirt and gather to 15½in (40cm) by pulling up the lower threads, making sure the gathers are evenly spaced.

3 Turn over ¼in (6mm) to the wrong side all around both waistband pieces and press the edges. Lay one waistband on top of the other, wrong sides together. Tuck rick-rack in between the two layers, with half of each 'scallop' protruding, and pin in place.

4 Fold a strap in half lengthways, tuck in the raw long edges and topstitch along the length, stitching as close to the edge as possible. Fold in the raw edges at one end. Repeat with the second strap. Tuck a strap into the waistband, under the rick-rack, at both ends. Sew the rick-rack, waistband and straps together on two sides and along the top, leaving the bottom edge open.

5 Now fit the gathered skirt inside the waistband, adjusting the gathers if necessary. Pin and tack in place. Topstitch along the front of the waistband, stitching as close to the edge as possible.

6 Double hem the bottom of the apron skirt (see page 131), turning over ¼in (6mm) and then ⅜in (1cm) to the wrong side press, and hem by hand (see page 136). Pin the pocket to the apron and stitch it in place.

Butcher's Apron

A striped apron shows that you mean business in the kitchen or at the barbecue. This is a classic shape, kept simple and ready to be embellished with personal touches such as a top pocket for the chef's spectacles, embroidered initials or a stencilled slogan.

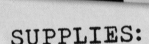

CUTTING LIST:

15 APRON
Cut one

16 STRAP
Cut three (not needed if you use apron tape for the straps)

17 LOOP
Cut one (not needed if you use apron tape for the straps)

18 BIB FACING
Cut one

19 POCKET
Cut one (with the stripes running horizontally)

SUPPLIES:

Patterns 15–19 from pattern sheet D

lyd (lm) striped heavy-duty fabric such as denim or canvas

1 set of D-rings

1in (2.5cm) apron tape (optional instead of sewn straps)

Basic sewing kit (see page 122)

Instructions:

1 Turn the apron sides over to the wrong side by ¼in (6mm) and then ½in (12mm), pressing the hem as you go and pinning to hold the shape.

2 Fold the three straps in half lengthways, then tuck the long raw edges in by ¼in (6mm) and press flat. At one end of each strap, fold the corners in to the middle to make a pointed end, then tuck in the raw edges. Machine stitch along the pointed end and the long edge, as close to the edge as possible. Make the loop

in the same way, but without a pointed end, thread the two D-rings onto it and then sew the two ends together.

3 Slip the raw ends of one strap under the side hem, just below the curve of the bib. Repeat on the other side. Now sew both side hems, close to the edge. Double hem the bottom of the apron by turning over ½in (12mm) and then 1½in (4cm) to the wrong side and machine stitch. Fold the straps back over the side hems and stitch them down flat.

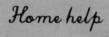

Home help

Use a heavy-duty (denim weight) needle. Slow right down when sewing through several layers, as this will help avoid needle breakage.

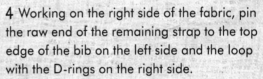

4 Working on the right side of the fabric, pin the raw end of the remaining strap to the top edge of the bib on the left side and the loop with the D-rings on the right side.

5 Overlap them with the bib facing. Line up the top edge, allowing an equal overlap on both sides. Pin, then sew slowly along the top edge.

6 Turn the apron to the wrong side of the fabric and bring the facing over to the back. Tuck in the side edges, fold up a hem to match the shape of the bib front and pin in place. Sew all the way around to outline the shape and reinforce the straps.

7 Zig-zag stitch the raw edges of the pocket, then fold down a 1in (2.5cm) hem at the top. Pin, then stitch the pocket to the apron below waist level. Sew a line of stitching down the centre of the pocket to divide it in two.

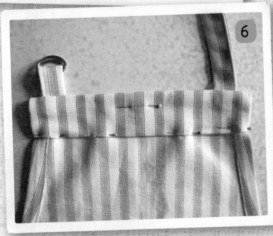

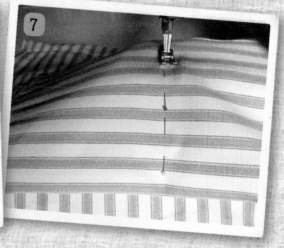

Plastic Bag Keeper

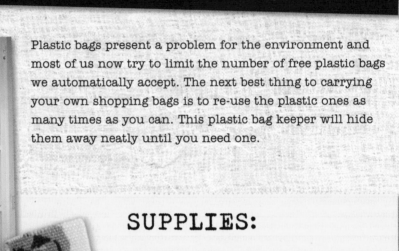

Plastic bags present a problem for the environment and most of us now try to limit the number of free plastic bags we automatically accept. The next best thing to carrying your own shopping bags is to re-use the plastic ones as many times as you can. This plastic bag keeper will hide them away neatly until you need one.

SUPPLIES:

18 x 30in (45 x 75cm) fabric

8in (20cm) elastic, 6mm wide

1yd (1m) ¼in (5mm) cord

Basic sewing kit (see page 122)

Safety pin for threading

Home help

Use a fabric you really love for this simple project and it will make you smile each time you re-use a bag.

Instructions:

1 Turn over ½in (12mm) to the wrong side at one short end of your fabric and press, folding the corners over in a triangle shape to tuck away the raw edges.

2 Tuck under the raw edge, pin, then machine stitch very close to the folded edge. This will form a channel for the elastic, so make sure it is wide enough. Repeat steps 1 and 2 at the other short end of the fabric. This will be the top where the drawstring cord is threaded through to close the bag and hang it up.

3 Turn over a small hem along each long edge and zig-zag stitch along the edge. Fold the fabric in half lengthways, wrong sides together, then pin and machine stitch the long side seam.

4 At the base of the holder, pin one end of the elastic to the seam to prevent it from pulling through. Attach a safety pin to the other end and thread it through the channel.

5 Check that the elastic hasn't twisted, then hand stitch the two ends together.

6 Thread the cord through the top channel and tie the ends together. Turn the bag keeper right side out. Use the cord to close the top and hang the bag keeper at a convenient height.

Bedroom

Nightdress or Pyjama Case

A long time ago, ladies had time to sit and embroider their initials on bed linen and make dressing table sets and pretty tray cloths for tea time. We can honour them by recycling their needlework into something that will have a special place in our lives.

Colourful embroidered flowers, cutwork lace and cross-stitch designs all work well for this project. If you are lucky enough to have heirloom pieces, they are better used than stored away out of sight; otherwise search in charity shops, antique linen shops or the online marketplace.

CUTTING OUT:

Measure the embroidered cloth and cut the lining fabric 1in (2.5cm) larger.

SUPPLIES:

Vintage hemmed cloth, approx. 18in (46cm) square

Fine cotton, silk or satin lining fabric in contrasting colour

Press stud, button or ribbon to fasten

Basic sewing kit (see page 122)

Instructions:

1 Turn over ½in (12mm) on all sides of the lining fabric, tuck the raw edge under and press flat. Pin, tack and slipstitch around all sides, using small stitches for a very neat finish.

2 Place the embroidered cloth on top of the lining, with the hemmed side facing upwards, and pin in place. Tack the two layers together, using a contrasting colour of thread.

3 Sew the embroidered cloth and lining together, either by machine or by hand, depending on the vintage cloth you are using. I used a machine, with white thread on top and lilac below – both cotton threads. Press well.

Home help

A lace edge may need to be 'eased' to fit the length. Work slowly to pin the two together and use more pins than usual.

4 Place the fabric embroidered side down then turn it around so that it makes a diamond shape. Fold the bottom point of the diamond in to the centre of the square then repeat with the two side points, making sure that the folded-in edges butt up against each other. Pin across the seams to hold the folds in place.

5 Turn the piece inside out and re-position the pins on the inside to close the lining seams. Whipstitch the edges together, using small neat stitches and stitching only across the edges of the lining fabric.

6 Attach your chosen fastener. You can use a press stud, ribbon, button and loop or button; select the type that best suits the weight of your fabric.

Travel Shoebag

Steal an idea from little kids taking their sports kit to school and make yourself a shoe bag. It's a neat way to pack shoes for travelling or to store them dust-free at home – and there's even an internal pocket for socks or tights as a bonus!

Scarves are ideal for this project, because they already have hems so the edges will not fray. Vintage souvenir scarves are perfect for the travel theme, but a bandana may suit men's or sports shoes better than vintage silk.

SUPPLIES:

1 scarf per pair of shoes

2in (5cm) square of iron-on hem fix

Ribbon twice the width of the scarf for the drawstring, ¾in (2cm) wide

2 buttons, 1–1½in (2.5–4cm) in diameter

Basic sewing kit (see page 122)

Instructions:

1 Cut the square of iron-on hem fix in half diagonally. Fold the two top corners of the scarf over to the wrong side to make a triangle and place the long side of the iron-on hem fix in the fold. Press with a warm iron to bond.

2 Along the top edge, fold over 1in (2.5cm) to the wrong side, press and pin in place. Machine stitch close to the edge. This forms the channel for the drawstring.

3 Place the scarf right side down on your work surface. Measure one of your shoes against it and allow a shoe length and a half for the bag, then turn the excess over at the base to make the inner pockets. Press the fold, then fold the scarf in half widthways and press again. Open out the widthways fold and pin along the crease line.

4

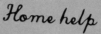

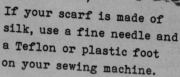

Home help

If your scarf is made of silk, use a fine needle and a Teflon or plastic foot on your sewing machine.

5

4 Pin along the bottom and up the side, stopping when you reach the top hem, leaving the two slanted openings for the drawstring. Machine stitch the seams. Remove all pins. Turn the bag right side out. Re-insert pins along the centre crease line, making sure the creases align on both sides of the bag, and machine stitch along the crease to make the internal pockets.

5 Thread the ribbon through the channel at the top of the bag and gather the bag to close it.

6 Finally, sew a button onto each ribbon end to prevent it from being pulled through the drawstring channel.

6

Padded Coat Hanger

There are many reasons why a padded hanger is better than wire or plastic and one of the best is that clothes stay put and don't slither off the minute you turn your back on them. They help keep shoulders in shape and also add a pretty, feminine touch of luxury to your wardrobe. Men's clothes need pampering, too, and hangers look good covered with fabric harvested from a worn checked shirt.

SUPPLIES:

2½in (6.5cm) wadding, 90in (228cm) wide

Multi-purpose glue or heavy-duty stapler

Wooden hanger

39 × 6in (100 × 15cm) light cotton or silk feature fabric

1 × 10in (2.5 × 25cm) feature fabric or 10in (25cm) ribbon, 1in (2.5cm) wide, for bow

Basic sewing kit (see page 122)

Home help

Traditionally, coat hanger covers have been made of fabric from worn-out dresses or leftovers from other sewing projects.

Instructions:

1 Glue or staple one end of the strip of wadding to the end of the hanger. Wrap it around the hanger, overlapping a little at each turn, until the hanger is completely covered. Cut off any excess wadding and secure the end in place with a few stitches.

2 With right sides together, fold the fabric in half lengthways and sew the short edges together.

3 Turn right side out and press under a hem of ½in (12mm) along both long raw edges.

Home help

If you don't have wadding, use tights (panty hose). They work just as well and you will have the satisfaction of doing some recycling.

4 Work a row of small running stitches along the folded edge, about ¼in (6mm) from the edge. Repeat along the open top edge to join the layers together, stopping just before you reach the centre.

5 Slip the hanger into the completed end, then finish the running stitch along the top edge. Gather up to fit and tie off the threads.

6 Fold the fabric for the bow in half lengthways, then tuck in all raw edges and machine stitch down both short sides and the long open edge. Tie in a bow around the base of the hook; alternatively, use a length of matching ribbon.

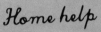

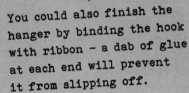

Home help

You could also finish the hanger by binding the hook with ribbon – a dab of glue at each end will prevent it from slipping off.

Eye Mask

CUTTING LIST:

20 **MASK**

Cut one in outer fabric, one in backing fabric and two in brushed cotton or flannelette for the filling

21 **STRAP**

Cut one in outer fabric

BINDING

24 × 2½in (60 × 6cm) bias-cut outer fabric

There are times when even a chink of light is too much. Be prepared and make those moments a little more self-indulgent by making yourself a silky eye mask.

The black fabric is hidden beneath the floral fabric, so there is no need to look like the Lone Ranger – unless you want to, of course, and in that case you can use black on the outside as well.

SUPPLIES:

Patterns 20–21 from pattern sheet E

½yd (50cm) outer fabric

5 × 9in (12.5 × 23cm) soft black cotton or silk for backing

10 × 9in (25 × 23cm) brushed cotton or flannelette for filling

24in (60cm) home-made or store-bought bias binding, 2½in (6cm) wide

12in (30cm) elastic, ¼in (6mm) wide

Basic sewing kit (see page 122)

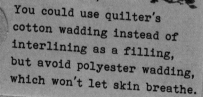

Home help

You could use quilter's cotton wadding instead of interlining as a filling, but avoid polyester wadding, which won't let skin breathe.

Instructions:

1 Layer the eye mask pieces, with the black backing fabric right side down on the bottom, the brushed cotton or flannelette filling in the middle and the outer fabric right side up on the top. Pin, then tack the layers together.

2 Prepare the bias strip if you are making your own (see page 149). Press each long raw edge under by ¼in (6mm).

3 Fold the strap in half lengthways, wrong sides together, and press. Fold under each long raw edge by ¼in (6mm) and sew along the long open edge, leaving a channel wide enough to take the elastic. Attach a safety pin to one end of the elastic and thread it through the channel, gathering up the fabric to fit the length. Stitch the elastic to each end of the strap to secure it in place.

Home help

I used reclaimed interlining as the filling for this eye mask, although any soft and lightweight natural fabric will do.

4 Open up the bias binding and pin it to the front of the mask, right sides together, aligning the raw edges. Tack in place. Machine stitch along the first crease line in the binding; where the two ends of binding meet, overlap one on the other to give a neat finish.

5 Turn the mask over and pin the ends of the strap to the side edges. Fold the binding tape over the straps, tucking in the raw edge and pinning it as you go. Keep checking the front to make sure that the binding is an even width all the way around. Using small backstitches, hand stitch the binding to the black backing.

6 When you've finished, fold the straps back level with the edge of the binding and machine stitch across them to secure them firmly in place.

Jewellery Roll

Keep all your jewellery together for travelling by making one of these rolls with a place for everything. There are a variety of pockets, so you can choose the compartments that best suit your own needs and follow the general instructions. Please note: there is no pocket for a tiara, so princesses will have to make other arrangements!

SUPPLIES:

Patterns 22–26 from pattern sheet E

¹/₂yd (50cm) outer fabric

¹/₂yd (50cm) lining fabric

9 × 1in (20 × 2.5cm) wadding

7in (18cm) zip

Small piece of hook-and-loop tape, ¹/₂in (12mm) wide

¹/₂yd (50cm) narrow ribbon for ties

2 press studs

3yd (3m) bias binding

Basic sewing kit (see page 122)

CUTTING LIST:

22 SMALL POCKETS
Cut two in outer fabric and two in lining fabric

23 RING HOLDER
Cut one in lining fabric and one in wadding

24 ZIPPED POCKET
Cut one in outer fabric and one in lining fabric

25 OPEN POCKET
Cut one in lining fabric

26 MAIN PIECE
Cut one in outer fabric and one in lining fabric

Instructions:

1 Place the two pieces for the zipped pocket wrong sides together, with the outer fabric on top. Fold under one long edge of both pieces by ¼in (6mm) and press. Pin this long edge to one edge of the zip tape, as close to the teeth as possible, taking care not to overlap the fabric onto the zip teeth. Using a zipper foot on your machine, stitch the zip in place (see page 141).

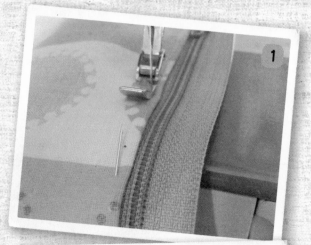

2 Turn under and press ¼in (6mm) to the wrong side along each long raw edge of the open pocket. Stitch a line down the centre to divide the pocket in two. Machine stitch one edge to form a neat hem. Pin and stitch the other edge to the other side of the zip tape from the previous step.

3 Trim about ¼in (6mm) off the length and width of the wadding and roll the ring holder fabric around it. Tuck in the raw seam edges, pin, then sew along the seam. Sew the hook side of the hook-and-loop tape to one end of the ring holder. Pin the other end to the long edge approx. 3½in (9cm) from the right-hand corner. Sew the other side of the hook-and-loop tape to the lining, making sure that it aligns with the hook side.

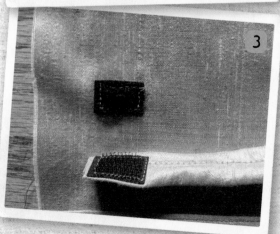

4 Place one outer and one lining small pocket piece right sides together and machine stitch around the edges, leaving the short straight end open. Turn under the short raw edges and topstitch. With wrong sides together, fold the pocket in half lengthways, leaving the flap protruding, and topstitch around the sides and base. Sew one piece of the press stud to the flap and the other to the front of the pocket. Repeat with the remaining pieces. Now topstitch the two pockets in place.

5 Fold the ribbon in half and sew it to the centre of the outer main piece on the right side. Place the outer main piece right side down on your work surface, with the lining fabric right side up on top.

6 Open up the bias binding and pin it to the lining side of the jewellery roll, right sides together, aligning the raw edges. Tack in place. Machine stitch along the first crease line in the binding, folding the binding in neatly at the corners; where the two ends of binding meet, overlap one on the other to give a neat finish.

7 Fold the binding over to the front of the jewellery roll and slipstitch it in place by hand.

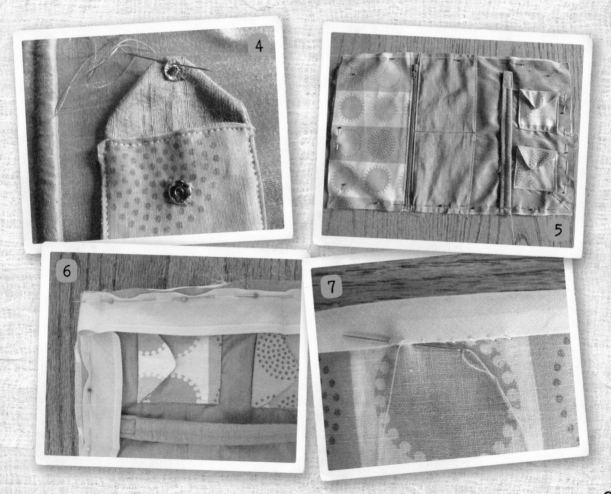

Bathroom

Wash Bag

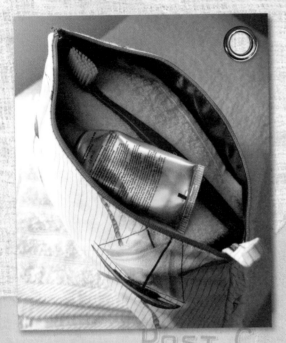

Styles change and it's not always easy to find that special wash bag when you are actually looking for one. The joy of home sewing is that if you make a wash bag it can be any size, colour and pattern you like. Choose fabric that you love and give it a practical waterproof lining. When you tire of it, make another one.

CUTTING LIST:

27 OUTERS
Cut two in outer fabric

28 LINING
Cut one on the fold in waterproof polyester fabric

LOOP
3 × 1in (7.5 × 2.5cm)
Cut one in outer fabric

SUPPLIES:

Patterns 27 and 28 from pattern sheet E

1/2yd (50cm) outer fabric

1/2yd (50cm) waterproof polyester fabric (a shower curtain is good)

8in (20cm) zip

Basic sewing kit (see page 122)

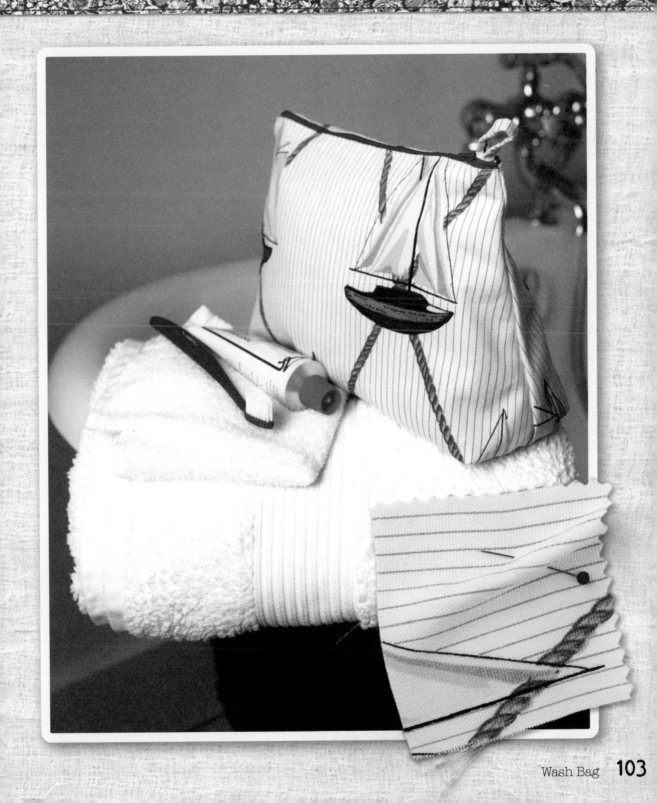

Instructions:

1 Along one long edge of both outer fabric pieces fold over ½in (12mm) and press to the wrong side. Following the instructions on page 141 and using a zipper foot on your machine, pin, tack and slowly machine stitch the zip in place. It helps to undo the zip for the first 2in (5cm) or so, then stop, pull it back up, and continue.

2 Fold the outer piece in half, right sides together. Pin and machine stitch the side seams, using a ¼in (6mm) seam. Press the seam open. Undo the zip, then stitch the base seam and press the seam open. Align the base and side seams, pinch out 2in (5cm) at each corner and pinch the two layers together to form a triangle. Stitch across the triangle 2in (5cm) from the tip, then trim away the excess. Turn the bag right side out.

3 Fold the lining fabric in half and sew up the side seams. Stitch and trim the corners of the base, as in step 3, but leave the lining piece right side out.

Home help

If you are new to sewing zips, it's a good idea to pin and then tack them in place using a contrasting thread and long running stitches.

4 Fold the fabric for the loop in half lengthways and press, tuck under the raw long edges and machine stitch along the open long edge. Sew the loop ends to the inner seam of the bag ½in (12mm) from the top, with the loop at the slider end of the zip.

5 Tuck the lining inside the outer bag, wrong sides together. Turn under the raw edges along the top of the lining and pin, then tack them in place.

6 Sew the lining to the outer bag either using a zipper foot on your machine or by hand using a neat slipstitch with the loop protruding at the slider end.

Laundry Bag

It's official: there is no end to laundry. The sense of achievement that you feel when the washing is done is very soon replaced by amazement at where the next load has come from.

Never fear: this big duffle bag will hang from a hook and hide it all away until you're ready to sling it over your shoulder, Brando-style, and go feed the machine.

CUTTING LIST:

BAG
24 x 30in (60 x 75cm)
Cut one in denim or canvas

LOOPS
2 x 4in (5 x 10cm)
Cut two in denim or canvas

Home help

The size of eyelets refers to the hole size. They come with their own assembly tool and instructions.

SUPPLIES:

1yd (1m) striped denim or canvas ticking

2yd (2m) soft piping cord, ¼in (6mm) thick

Pack of ½in (14mm) brass eyelets

Basic sewing kit

Ruler

Marker pen

Hammer

Instructions:

1 Fold the fabric in half lengthways, wrong sides together. Pin and machine stitch along each side, using a ¼in (6mm) seam. Trim the seam allowance and press the seam open.

2 Turn the bag inside out and press along the stitching line from the previous step. Repeat step 1, pinning and sewing another ¼in (6mm) seam. This makes a very strong, neat, no-fray seam, known as a French seam.

3 Now using a ruler and marker pen, draw a 3in (7.5cm) square in each bottom corner of the bag.

4 Aligning the base and side seams, pinch the two layers together to form a triangle. Using the drawn line as a guide, stitch across the triangle, then trim away the excess to a neat ½in (12mm). Turn the bag right side out.

5 Turn the top edge of the bag over to the wrong side twice by 1½in (4cm) and then again. Machine stitch close to the edge.

6 Mark the positions of the eyelets: you need at least four along the front and four along the back. Cut a cross, then trim away to make a hole slightly smaller than the eyelet hole.

7 Insert the eyelets, following the instructions on the pack (see page 146). Work on a hard surface and give the eyelet tool a few good whacks with the hammer.

8 Thread the cord through the eyelets, with the ends facing the front. Make a pair of loops by folding and topstitching two small pieces of matching fabric, and then sewing them to the back edge of the bag so that you can hang it up.

Bath Cap

CUTTING LIST:

㉙ MAIN PIECE

Cut one on the fold in outer fabric and one on the fold in lining fabric

BIAS BINDING

Cut a length the circumference of the circle plus 1in (2.5cm)

Taking a bath doesn't always involve a hair wash: sometimes we want to refresh or relax and emerge with our hairstyle intact. This is when the bath cap is called into play – but it is difficult to find one that will add style to your bath-time look.

Choose a fabric that you adore and run up this little number to make you feel a bit more glamorous in the tub or the shower.

SUPPLIES:

Pattern 29 from pattern sheet F

½yd (50cm) outer fabric

¹/₂yd (50cm) waterproof soft polyester fabric for the lining

2yd (2m) bias binding tape

¹/₂yd (50cm) soft elastic, ¹/₄in (6mm) wide

Basic sewing kit (see page 122)

Home help

Soft waterproof polyester can be bought online. Alternatively, use a cheap shower curtain; high-quality ones are too thick.

Instructions:

1 Place the outer and lining circles on top of each other, wrong sides together. Pin near the edge at the cardinal points (north, south, east and west). Working with the lining fabric on top, open out one folded edge of the bias binding, place it right side down around the edge, then pin along the fold line, overlapping the ends.

2 Tack along the fold line in a contrasting colour of thread, removing the pins as you go.

3 Machine stitch carefully along the tacked line, turning the raw ends of the binding under as you complete the circle.

4 Next, fold the binding over to the other side to enclose both fabrics and pin in place. Tack and machine stitch.

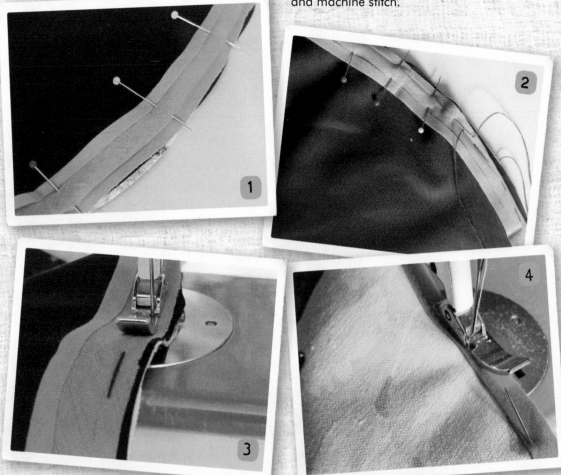

5 Pinch and pin the fabric into pleats 1in (2.5cm) deep at the cardinal points, then pin more pleats in between, spacing them evenly. Pin them flat 1in (2.5cm) from the edge.

6 Now measure the elastic around your head, stretching it as you go. It has to stay put but not pinch. Cut the elastic to length and pin one end inside a pleat 1½in (4cm) down from the outer edge. Stretch and pin the elastic all the way around the circle, then tack it in place. Slowly and carefully machine stitch the elastic in place, using a zig-zag stitch, stretching the elastic with one hand while guiding the fabric with the other as you sew. When the tension is released, the cap will gather up with a pretty, frilled edge.

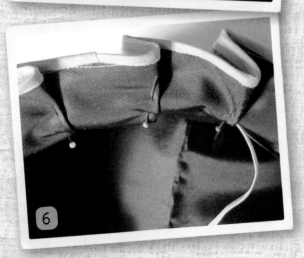

Home help

It's a little tricky to stitch the elastic in place, so it's a good idea to practise on a scrap of fabric first.

Hairstyling Bag

This cute bucket bag keeps all your hairdressing bits and pieces in one place. Choose a fabric with some structure, such as an upholstery-weight linen, or interline the bag with strong canvas so that it keeps its shape. Design the inside pockets and elastic to suit your own styling needs.

SUPPLIES:

Patterns 30–35 from pattern sheet F

½yd (50cm) outer fabric

½yd (50cm) lining fabric

Oddments of fabric for inner pockets

½yd (50cm) elastic

1in (2.5cm) wide 6in (15cm) zip

1yd (1m) petersham tape or strip of strong canvas, 1in (2.5cm) wide

Basic sewing kit (see page 122)

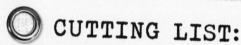

CUTTING LIST:

30 STRAP
Cut two in outer fabric and two in lining fabric

31 OUTER POCKET
Cut one in outer fabric and one in lining fabric

32 LARGER INNER POCKET
Cut one in oddment or lining fabric

33 SIDES
Cut one in outer fabric and one in lining fabric

34 BASE
Cut one in outer fabric and one in lining fabric

35 COMB POCKET
Cut one in oddment or lining fabric

Instructions:

1 Stretch the elastic around your usual hairstyling products to decide how long it needs to be for the stretchy loop and add 1in (2.5cm). Turn under each end of the elastic by ½in (12mm), pin the loop in place on the lining and machine stitch in place.

2 Hem the large inner pocket all around and press. Place the pocket right side down, and pin and tack one edge of the zip tape right side down along the top edge. Machine stitch

in place, using a zipper foot. Pin and machine stitch the pocket right side up to the bag lining, stitching along the long edge of the zip tape and around the sides and base of the pocket to fix it in place. At this stage, you can customize the bag to your own requirements.

3 With right sides together, begin fitting the bottom edge of the lining to the base lining, easing it into place and pinning as you go. Tack the base to the lining. Pin and sew up the side seam. Sew slowly around the base, taking care to follow the curve. Repeat with the outer fabric bag and base.

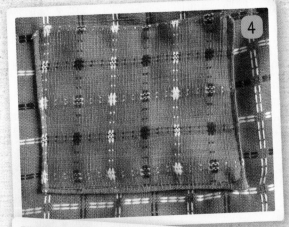

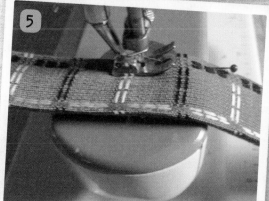

4 Place the outer and lining fabrics for the outside pocket right sides together and machine stitch around three sides. Turn right side out, turn under and press the raw edge and stitch the pocket to the outside fabric.

5 Turn under ¼in (6mm) along each long edge of the outer and inner fabric strap and press. Place the straps wrong sides together, with a strip of petersham ribbon or canvas in the middle to reinforce, and topstitch around all four sides. Repeat to make the second strap. Turn over the top edge of the outer bag by 1in (2.5cm), place a strip of reinforcing ribbon or canvas inside the fold and machine stitch in place.

6 Pin the handle ends in position on the inside top edge of the outer bag. Slip the lining in place, aligning the seams with those of the outer bag, and topstitch around the top of the bag to secure all the layers together.

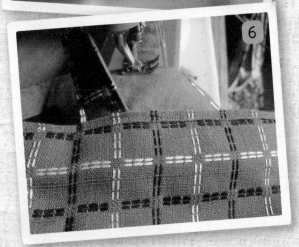

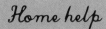

Home help

The reinforcing around the neck of the bag and handle is not visible, but it makes the bag much more sturdy.

Supplies & Techniques

Retro-style & Recycled Fabrics

Finding vintage fabric takes time and dedication, and searching it out can become a bit of an obsession. If you have neither the time nor the inclination to get that deeply involved, you can still get the retro look. Choose your fabrics and trimmings carefully and do a bit of research and you'll find it surprisingly easy to create an authentic-looking retro piece.

Recycling fabric

There is more than enough fabric in the world already and you'd be amazed by the amount that goes into landfill. So, try to re-use fabric wherever possible by re-working old curtains, tablecloths or clothing. Alternatively, try to buy vintage fabrics for your projects.

Natural fabrics are particularly appropriate if you're going for a retro look. Natural fabrics come from living things and include cotton, linen, silk, wool and plant fibres such as bamboo or hemp. Their qualities are quite predictable – and best of all, they are 100% biodegradable.

Genuine vintage fabrics come from all sorts of places and most will need a good wash and press. Even clean fabrics can smell musty or reek of fabric conditioner, so it's best to wash and press them before you embark on a sewing project.

One problem with vintage cottons and linens is that they fade because the dyes that were used were less fast. If you are using genuine vintage fabric, do check its quality before you spend hours sewing, because fading can also be a sign of deterioration. The same applies to colour fastness – it's a good idea to check the fabric before you embark on any sewing. Dip a corner of the fabric into a bowl of hot water and agitate: if the water stays clear, you're fine; if it does not, think again.

Go Green

It's now possible to buy recycled sewing thread, so ask your supplier to stock it and help get it into the mainstream.

Before you spend any money at all on fabric, have a look around the house. Old cotton sheets make good linings and can be dyed to suit your colour scheme. Curtains can be transformed into cushions or bags, blankets make cozy cushion covers and dress and shirt fabrics can be combined in patchwork throws.

Fabric production can be unfriendly to the environment, so go for organic and fairly traded options whenever you can.

Look out for vintage fabrics in charity shops, flea markets and at car boot sales.

If you can't bear the idea of sorting through other people's cast-offs, then look online. Auction sites have a constantly changing supply of old curtains, tablecloths, shirts and bedcovers.

Buying retro-style fabrics

New ranges of old designs come out with every season and this applies at every level, from frighteningly expensive upholstery fabrics to cheap and cheerful poly-cottons. There are plenty of atomic patterns from the 1950s, bright swirls and geometrics from the '60s as well as more historic textiles such as feedsack linens, woven plaids, tickings and traditional tweeds.

New fabrics printed with modern chemical dyes hold on to their strong colours. There are also now ready-faded, imitation vintage fabrics in all the old patterns, which allows us to fast-track to the look without having to search out the real thing. When buying new cotton or linen, ask for pre-shrunk fabric, otherwise it may shrink in the wash.

Basic Sewing Kit

A custom-designed sewing basket has a place for everything, but you don't actually need one before you start sewing. Any box will do: for a real retro vibe, use an old biscuit tin. Most importantly, keep whatever you use tidy. Pins and needles can be kept on a pincushion and threads in a see-through box. The following list will see you through most sewing projects.

Sewing machine

Old machines were made of metal and solidly engineered. If used regularly and serviced, they should last a lifetime. Many people who learn on old machines prefer to stick with them.

New sewing machines are lighter, as many metal parts have been replaced with plastic, which makes them more likely to vibrate and move as you sew. On the plus side, the motors are quieter and many machines are computerized with easy-to-use buttonhole and embroidery patterns.

A lightweight, inexpensive machine will be fine for most home sewing projects, but curtains or soft furnishings may need a sturdier model that is able to stitch through several layers of fabric. Buy the best machine you can afford. Most come with a range of different presser feet; the other essential is a zipper foot for zippers and piping.

Choose your machine to suit your needs – but bear in mind that you may become more ambitious as your confidence grows.

Machine needles

All machines will have a recommendation on which needles to use and there are also universal needles that fit most machines. Don't go for the cheapest needles, as they may have rough edges that can rip the fabric. Broadly speaking, the needle sizes should correspond with the weight of the fabric you are using. Always test your needle on a scrap of the fabric you're using for your project to make sure it's suitable: if you use a thick, heavy needle on a sheer fabric such as organza, you're likely to end up with holes in it.

Sewing machine needle sizes

	American		European	
Lightest	8		60	Lightest
	9		65	
	10		70	
	11		75	
	12		80	
	14		90	
	16		100	
	18		110	
Heaviest	19		120	Heaviest

Needles for hand sewing

A pack of assorted needles is all you need
to get started. Needle sizes range from 1 to
10, with the largest being No 1. They have
traditional names. Sharps are the most
commonly used. They are small eyed, medium-
length needles that are used for most hand
sewing. Tapestry needles are blunt ended
and long eyed, and used for canvas work.
Embroidery needles are sharp with long
eyes for threading the stranded silk threads.
Milliner's needles are sharp, long, and useful
for tacking.

Pins

Blunt pins can damage fabric,
so treat yourself to new, sharp
pins. Those with glass or plastic heads
are easy to use and visible, so less likely to
be left in your work. Old packets of pins from
antique workboxes look good, but most will be
rusty and blunt. Keep pins on a pincushion
with the points out of harm's way. Extra-long
quilter's pins are useful for pinning several
layers together.

Tape measure

Whether you are working in yards or metres, you will always need a tape measure close to hand. A ruler is also useful.

Scissors

Buy the most expensive pair of dressmaker's scissors that you can afford and you will not regret the money spent. Cheap scissors will soon go blunt and frustrate your efforts to cut accurately. Buy one large pair and a pair of embroidery scissors for cutting threads and detailed work. Also invest in a medium-sized, less expensive pair of scissors for cutting paper patterns. Never use your best dressmaker's scissors for cutting paper patterns, as they will quickly blunt.

Pinking shears produce a zig-zagged edge, which is less likely to fray and can be useful for finishing seams (see page 134). They are, however, not suitable for all types of fabric.

Seam ripper or unpicker

This is a very simple, useful gadget. One end is forked, with a bead on the longer point and a sharp point set further back. It is inserted between layers of fabric to cut through stitches for quick unpicking. It is also the very best tool for cutting buttonholes.

Tailor's chalk

Tailor's chalk is made of compressed chalk and has a sharp edge that is used to mark fabric for sewing. It brushes off easily and comes in white and colours; a fadeaway fabric marker pen is a good alternative.

Thimble

Sewing by hand involves pushing the blunt end of the needle through the fabric many times and a thimble guards against tender spots.

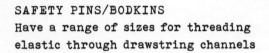

Useful Extras

The following are not essential, but they do make life a little easier when you're sewing! As you get more experienced, you will undoubtedly come across other gadgets that you may want to add to your collection.

NEEDLE THREADER
These little gadgets are useful for those with poor eyesight.

SAFETY PINS/BODKINS
Have a range of sizes for threading elastic through drawstring channels

FUSIBLE BONDING WEB
Useful in appliqué work. Bond the shapes to the background fabric before stitching and it won't fray.

IRON-ON HEM FIX
Not only does the tape bond the hem, bit it also gives a nice crisp edge.

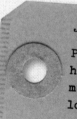

Threads

Stock your sewing kit with a selection of coloured threads, plus a large reel each of black, white and cream. Old spools of thread look great, but they are best kept for display as they are likely to break and cause a build-up of fluff in your sewing machine.

Both cotton and polyester threads are available. They come in a range of weights to suit different fabrics. Polyester thread is a man-made fibre and was designed for use on sewing machines. It has a slightly stretchy quality. Buy the best you can. Cotton is ideal for natural fabrics and come in much the same range of colours as polyester.

Home help
People who work in haberdashery stores are mostly there because they love sewing – they are a great source of advice.

Iron

An iron is absolutely essential for any sewing project, as you need to press seams open as you go (see page 135). If space allows, set up your ironing board and iron next to your sewing machine so you can easily move between the two.

Working with Patterns

Not every project in this book needs a paper pattern, but all of those that do can be found on the pull-out sheets at the back of the book. They are printed full size and ready to use. Simply choose the pattern pieces you need and trace them off. You'll have a pattern you can use again and again.

Tracing pattern pieces

The pattern sheets are printed on both sides, so you will need to trace the patterns off in order to use all of them.

First locate the pieces you need. Each project lists the piece numbers and the sheet to find them on in the Supplies list.

To trace the patterns, you can either lay transparent paper on top of the pattern sheets and trace the outline through it or use the carbon paper method. For this you'll need a dressmaker's tracing wheel and some carbon copy paper. Place the paper you want to trace onto (brown parcel paper is ideal) on your work surface, lay the carbon paper on top of it and the pattern sheet on top of that with the pattern facing up. Use the tracing wheel to trace round the pattern edges. When you take the carbon paper away your pattern piece will have been copied onto the bottom paper.

Cutting fabric

Lay the fabric on a flat surface and make sure that there are no creases. Press it smooth if necessary. Now lay the pattern pieces out on the fabric in the most economical way before you cut, so that any leftover fabric is in one useable piece.

If you find a pattern piece has a long red arrow marked 'Grainline', the arrow must align with the fabric's natural grain. Place the pattern piece with the arrow running parallel to the fabric's selvedge (the long, woven edge). Measure from the selvedge to each end of the arrow. If the distance is the same the pattern piece is running straight with the grainline.

The Cutting List for each project will tell you how many pieces to cut, and from which type of fabric. Pin the paper to the fabric and use sharp dressmaking shears to cut around the shape, cutting right up to the edge. Then remove the pattern and refold it so that you can use it another time.

Home help

When working with a washable recycled fabric, it is best to wash it before cutting out your pieces.

Making Your Own Patterns

If you have a much-loved item that has seen better days, such as an apron, cushion or bag, you can use your sewing skills to make another in its image.

If the item really has reached the end of its life, unpick the seams carefully and then press them flat. Place each fabric piece on brown parcel paper or tracing paper and draw around it. Take a note of any special features, such as openings or buttonholes.

Transfer them onto the fabric by inserting small-headed pins into the same place from the front and back. Remove the paper pattern carefully, leaving the pins in place, then replace the pins by marking the fabric with tailor's chalk or a fadeaway fabric marker.

If you would prefer the original item to remain intact, press it and place it on the paper. Draw around the shape, then tidy it up and add $^1/_2$in (12mm) all around the edges for the seam allowance.

Cutting 'on the fold'

Some patterns need to be cut out 'on the fold'. The fold line and the direction of the fabric's grain will be shown on the pattern if required. Fold the fabric in half widthways and line the fold line on the pattern with the folded edge. Pin the pattern in place, making sure you pin through both layers of fabric, and cut out the fabric as normal.

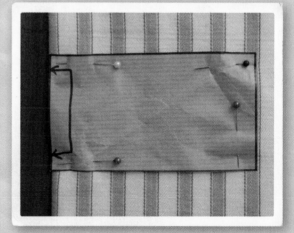

Machine Sewing

The invention of the sewing machine changed people's lives and there is still something rather life-changing about learning to use one in the 21st century. The basics remain the same: threads from above and below are locked together to make lines of stitching that hold fabrics together. How useful!

Before you sew

While it may be tempting to launch straight into your first project, taking a moment to set everything up properly will pay off and could save time, and fabric, later on.

When sewing, always sit comfortably with your back well supported and your feet touching the floor. An office chair on castors is a perfect sewing chair.

Fluff is the sewing machine's worst enemy. Check below the foot plate and clear it before you begin and regularly while sewing.

Always use the same type and weight of thread in the needle above and the bobbin below. Don't mix polyester and cotton.

Sew a few lines of practice stitching on scrap fabric before you begin. Problems with the tension are indicated by looped thread below or thread not being pulled up to form proper stitches. Consult your sewing machine manual on how to adjust the tension.

Home help

Sewing machines need oil to keep them running smoothly. Consult your handbook and follow the instructions.

Your first stitches

1 Lift the presser foot.

2 Place the fabric under it.

3 Pull the needle and the bobbin threads towards the back of your work, away from the needle – otherwise, they may tangle up with the stitches as you sew.

4 Position the needle on the fabric, then lower the presser foot.

5 Use the handwheel to lower the needle onto the fabric before applying pressure to the foot control – otherwise the jolt as you start can un-thread the needle.

6 Begin by 'locking' the seam. Sew forwards for a few stitches, then backwards over the stitches and then forwards again. Do the same at the other end.

Take it Slowly

Sewing machines don't like to be rushed. Any job that is done in a hurry will invariably go wrong in one of these three ways:

1) The bobbin will run out and you won't realize until you reach the end of the seam, when you discover that it has not been sewn.

2) The needle will break.

3) The tension, which has been perfect, will inexplicably re-adjust itself and produce a tangle beneath your work. Always unplug the machine before you investigate why it's stopped working. Basic tangles are easily sorted out by taking the bobbin casing out and pulling the threads clear of the mechanism.

Pinning, Tacking & Hemming

Don't be tempted to skip accurate pinning and tacking just because they are time-consuming. It really is worth the effort and will prevent the fabric from slipping out of position when you sew. Hemming is an essential skill for all sewing projects and there are several ways of achieving a neat finish.

Pinning

Sharp pins should be handled with care; when sewing by hand, insert the pins with their points facing away from you, so that you work towards the blunt end and can remove them before you catch your finger on them. If you do prick your finger, put your work aside until the danger of blood spots has passed.

A sewing machine can only stitch across pins that are inserted at a right angle to the stitching line but not across those that are in line with the needle. Remove the pins before they reach the sewing foot, as they will break the needle.

Tacking

Tacking creates a temporary hem that holds two or more layers together in preparation for sewing. This method is useful for inserting zips, matching patterns and sewing slippery fabrics such as satin.

Work tacking stitches in a contrasting colour of thread, so that they are easy to see and remove. Begin with a knotted thread and insert the needle from below. Take the needle back down and up again at regular intervals to make long running stitches and finish by securing the thread with a backstitch. Work slightly off the seam line to keep the tacked and machined stitches apart.

Hemming

Hems can be sewn either by hand or machine. The main advantage of hand sewing is that you can control the number of threads the needle picks up, making the stitching almost invisible on the right side. Hand-sewn hems on curtains can be deeper and the extra weight allows them to hang better than those that are machined.

Machined hems look best if they are shallow as there is less chance of the fabric shifting and puckering.

Fusible hem

Fusible hem is an iron-on tape that is inserted between the folded hem and the fabric, then pressed into place with a warm iron; follow the manufacturer's instructions. It is seen as an easy option but beware, as it can get messy! Make sure the tape is completely covered before you iron it in position; if any of it is left sticking out of the fold, it will fuse to the hotplate of the iron and it is very difficult to remove.

Hemming stitch

This is the most common form of hem stitch. From the right side of the work, hemming stitch is virtually invisible. It is worked from right to left.

1 Fold over the edge to be hemmed by ¼in (6mm), pin and press to tuck in the raw edge; then fold the hem again to the required depth.

2 Knot the thread to secure it and insert the needle under the fold, pulling it through to anchor it and hide the knot. Pick up a couple of threads from the fabric and insert the angled needle so it comes up in line with the point at which it first emerged. Repeat this along the hem, taking care to keep the length of stitches and the angle of the needle the same. Sew the final stitch twice to secure it.

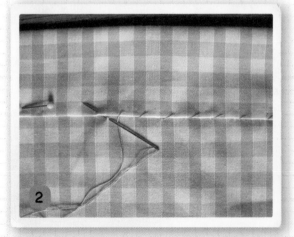

Herringbone stitch

This stitch has some 'give' and is good for stretchy fabric. It is worked from left to right.

Fold and pin the edge to be hemmed, as for hemming stitch (see page 131). Knot the thread to secure it and insert the needle under the fold, pulling it through to anchor it and hide the knot. Insert the needle a stitch width to the right and a short distance above the fold and pick up a few threads of fabric, with the needle parallel to the edge and pointing towards the right. Pull the needle through, then take it forward the same distance and do the same on the folded edge. Repeat to get the zig-zag effect.

Bound hem

A bound hem is half machined and half hand sewn. It is useful when fabric is limited or when you want to make a contrasting decorative edging. Use either ready-made bias binding or make your own (see page 149).

1 Unfold one side of the bias binding and pin it to the right side of the fabric, aligned with the fabric edge. Machine stitch along the first crease line.

2 Fold the tape over to the wrong side of the fabric, pin it in place and hem stitch by hand.

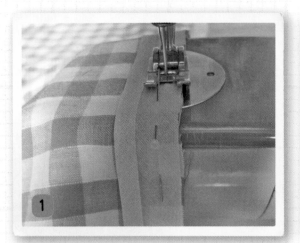

Finishing Seams

Just because seams are hidden on the inside, that doesn't mean they don't need some care and attention. Take the time to finish raw edges and press seams open so that they lie flat and your work will look neater and last longer.

Reducing seam bulk

When a fabric is heavy, the seams may appear too bulky and spoil the shape on the outside. Trimming back the seam allowance should solve this and you will find that the seams sit much flatter.

On straight seams, trim both seam allowances together to about half the original seam width (1).

A curved seam will need to be clipped to make the fabric lie flat. If the curve faces inwards, there will be too much seam allowance beyond the stitching line. Clip the seam allowance at regular intervals almost up to the stitching (2). This allows the snipped sections to overlap each other slightly to form a neater curve.

When the curve is outward facing, there is not enough fabric beyond the stitching line and it will pucker up. Snip V-shaped notches at regular intervals up to the stitching to allow the seam allowance to expand around the curve without any resistance (3).

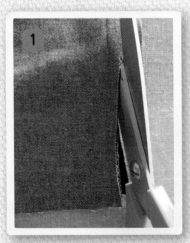
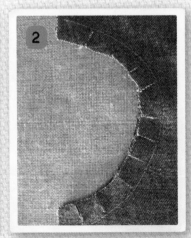
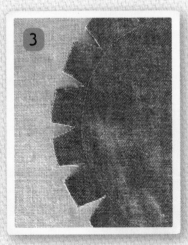

Neatening seams

A seam, once sewn, is visible on the outside as a neat line but the other side may not look as presentable. Most cut fabric will fray, some types more so than others – but by using one of the methods shown below, you can avoid getting too many straggly ends. These methods protect the seam from wear and tear, as well as neatening them.

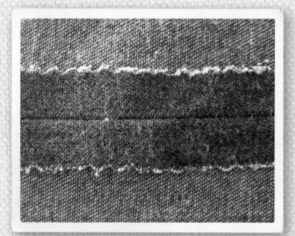

Pinked seam allowances

Pinking shears create a zig-zag edge that will not fray, but they don't work for all fabrics. They're best used on close-woven cotton and woollen materials or fabrics that don't fray such as felt and fleece.

Trim the edges of the seam allowances, cutting away as little fabric as possible and taking great care not to cut through the stitching.

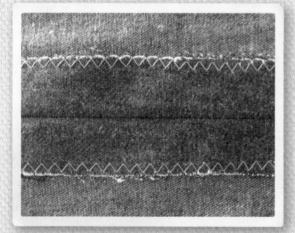

Zig-zagged seam allowances

This finish is suitable for most types of fabric. Commercially produced garments and curtains are finished off with a more complex version of zig-zag stitching using a machine called an overlocker; there are overlockers available for home use, but they're only really worth having if you intend to do a lot of sewing.

Work a line of zig-zag stitching along every edge of the seam allowance.

Oversewn seam allowances

If your machine doesn't do zig-zag stitching, you can overcast the edges of the seam allowances by hand.

Use small, loose stitches to overcast, taking the stitches over the edge of the seam allowance but not into the underlying fabric.

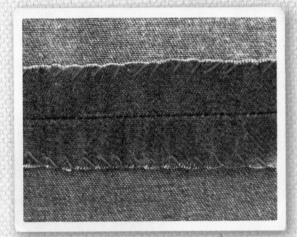

Pressing

Pressing is essential at all stages of the sewing process, before, during and after seams have been sewn. The important thing to remember is that pressing is not done in the same way as ironing: it is done with more of a lower-and-lift motion than a long, smoothing stroke.

A pressed fold or seam is so much easier to sew – and it cuts down on the amount of pins you need to use as well. Hems should never be attempted without first pressing the fold; even reluctant curves can be persuaded into shape with a warm iron.

Once a seam has been sewn, it can be pressed open on the wrong side of the fabric, this will eliminate any lumps and bumps. It can then be crossed by another seam with everything in the right place. It also helps you to see the shape of what you're making and make any adjustments as you go along.

Double check that the iron's heat setting suits your fabric, then press the seams open so that they lie flat, lowering the iron onto the fabric and then lifting it off again, rather than sliding it across the fabric as you do when ironing clothes.

Home help

Setting the ironing board up close to your sewing area will save a lot of time going back and forth.

Gathering

Retro styling loves a full skirt, be it on an apron or a dressing table. It harks back to the days when girls in full skirts and cinched waists jived to hip tunes on the jukebox.

How to use gathering

Gathering is a way of reducing the width of the top of a piece of fabric by pulling up a thread so that it falls with a soft fullness. Gathered edges are always sewn into a fixed binding or a waistband, such as, the waistband on a frilly apron or a binding on a lampshade. Gathering can also be used to soften edges and add plumpness to cushions. It doesn't always have to be a stand-out feature and can be a useful method for fitting fabric around corners in upholstery.

Hand-sewn gathering

1 Thread a needle with a knotted length of thread and sew running stitches along the top of the fabric. Do not backstitch the end, but leave it free. Sew a second row in the same way.

2 Pull both the ends of the thread in one direction while gathering the fabric in the other. Measure it against the fabric it is to fit. When the required width is reached, re-thread the needle and backstitch to lock the thread. Fit the gathered edge and stitching inside the binding or waistband, pin and topstitch.

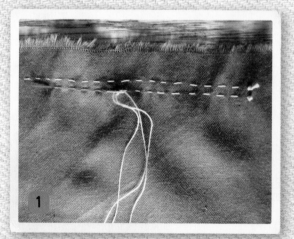

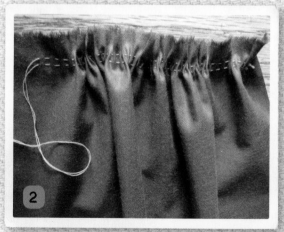

Machine gathering

1 Adjust the stitch width to the longest length and sew two rows of stitching, backstitching at the start of the rows but leaving a length of thread free at the ends.

2 Hold the fabric at the backstitched end while grasping the two bobbin (underneath) threads with the other hand. Pull the threads and move the gathering in the opposite direction until you reach the required width. Tie the threads together to stop them from unravelling.

3 Fit the gathered edge inside the binding or waistband, pin and topstitch.

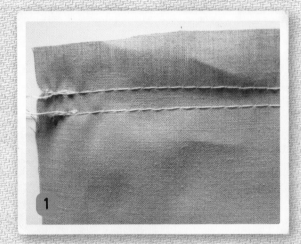

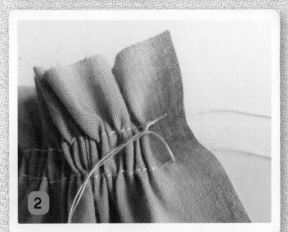

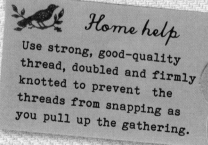

Home help

Use strong, good-quality thread, doubled and firmly knotted to prevent the threads from snapping as you pull up the gathering.

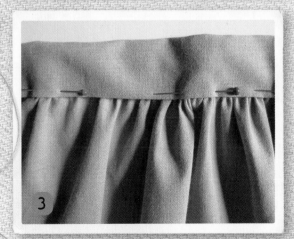

Fastenings

Most things we make require some sort of fastening and there are a number of options. Much depends on style and function: sometimes, a hidden fastening is preferable to a brightly coloured button.

Sewing on buttons

Buttons vary, but they are either of the shank type, where you sew through a raised eye at the back, or the flat type with holes for the thread. Flat buttons suit finer fabrics. Thicker materials need a shank to accommodate the depth of the fabric that is being buttoned through. Flat buttons will be more secure and look neater if you make a thread shank, as shown.

1 Knot the thread and push the needle up through the button from below. Keep the thread loose and return to the back and repeat. If there are four holes in the button you can either sew in two bars or make a cross. Slide a hairgrip between the button and the fabric and pull the threads tight. Sew through the button several times then bring the needle out below it.

2 Remove the hairpin and form a loop of thread around the button, take the needle through it and pull up tightly. Repeat several times to make the thread shank.

3 Take the needle through to the back of the work. Secure the end of the thread with several small stitches.

Buttonholes

The problem with a buttonhole is it that it is done at the end of the project – and a bad one can spoil the whole thing. Buttonholes can be worked by machine or by hand. The button dictates the size of the buttonhole, which is not cut until the stitching is complete. Closely worked stitching prevents the buttonhole's edges from fraying or tearing.

Home help

Make your buttonhole ¼in (6mm) larger than the button that it is being made for.

Machined butttonholes

Some sewing machines have a virtually foolproof buttonhole program, which makes life a lot easier! Others have four-stage buttonholes (marked A–D or 1–4) on a dial.

Always do a practice buttonhole using the same thread and fabric. Check that you have enough thread in the bobbin before you begin.

1 Mark the length and position of your buttonhole with tailor's chalk or pencil.

2 Turn the dial to buttonhole position A or 1. The arrow shows the stitching direction. Position the needle to begin on the left side of the buttonhole and sew up to the top.

Turn the dial to position B or 2. Sew at least four stitches across the top. Turn the dial to position C or 3. Position the needle on the inside and sew down to the bottom. Turn the dial to D or 4 and sew at least four stitches. Repeat all four steps for a stronger buttonhole.

Do not cut the thread between stages A and D or 1 and 4.

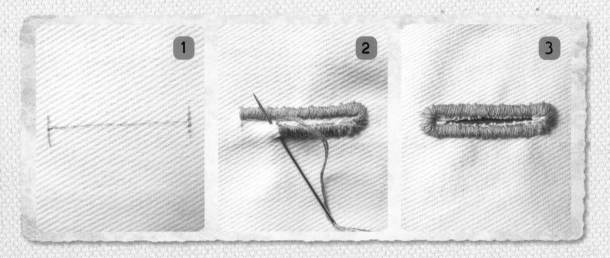

Hand-sewn buttonholes

Work buttonholes in satin stitch (see page 145) to make more of a feature, using two or three strands of embroidery silk in a matching or contrasting colour. Hand sewing has a charm of its own, so don't be too hard on yourself if your effort doesn't look like the machine version – that's the point!

1 Mark the position and length of the buttonhole on your fabric.

2 Knot the thread and begin from under the fabric, bringing the needle up just below the line and inserting it directly above (see satin stitch, page 145).

3 Try to keep the stitches neat and even, fanning them out as you turn the corners.

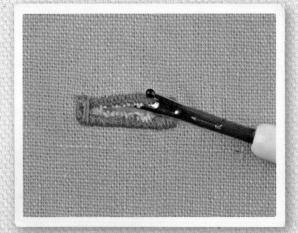

Cutting buttonholes

Cut buttonholes carefully so as not to slice through any of the stitching. A seam ripper is the ideal instrument to use. Poke the sharp end through the fabric at one end of the buttonhole and slide it along. Small, sharply pointed scissors can also be used. Trim away loose threads with care.

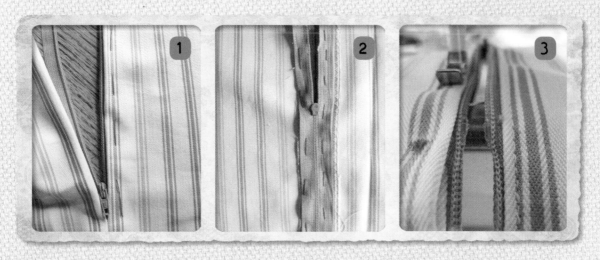

Zips

Measure the opening and buy a zip to fit rather than trying to fit the wrong size or style of zip, just because you have one.

1 Stitch the seam, leaving an opening the length of the zip. Tack the zip opening along the seamline and press open. Place the closed zip behind the tacked opening, then tack it to the seam allowance.

2 Fit the zipper foot to your machine and sew one side of the zip tape in place, with the zip closed.

3 Open the zip and sew the other side of the tape.

Hook-and-loop tape

There are two sides to this tape – one with nylon loops and the other a soft pile fabric.

To use hook-and-loop tape, cut a length of tape with both parts pressed together. Separate them and sew the hook half in place. Press the two fabrics together and, using the hook tape as a guide, mark the position for the loop part with two pins. Position the loop tape, remove the marker pins and sew it in place.

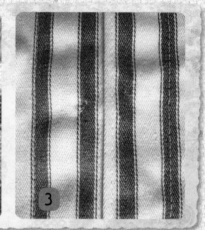

Hooks and eyes

Hooks and eyes are old fashioned and rather nice. They are often used for soft upholstery to join loose covers or to take the strain above a zipper.

1 Knot the thread and bring the needle up inside the ring of the eye. Insert the needle close to the outer edge, but don't pull the thread all the way through – leave a loop. Bring the needle up on the inside of the eye again.

Now pick the loop up with the needle and pull the thread down firmly to the fabric. Repeat, keeping the stitches close together.

2 Position the hook, using pins or a marker pen. Overlap the joining fabrics to avoid gaping between the fastenings.

3 The hooks and eyes should be invisible from the outside.

Press studs or poppers

These come in a range of sizes. They are useful for keeping flaps closed and attaching badges or other removable trimmings. To position the two halves accurately, sew the first one in place, then pop the other half onto it and insert a needle through both and into the fabric opposite.

Embroidery Stitches

Hundreds of books have been written about embroidery and, along with all other handicrafts, it's staging a come-back. Here are a few very simple stitches that can be used to add a personal touch.

Backstitch

This is both functional (it is the best hand stitch for sewing seams) and decorative (a really neat way of outlining embroidery motifs). Work from right to left.

Bring the needle up one stitch length from the end of the stitching line. Take it back down at the end of the stitching line and bring it up again one stitch length ahead of the point from which it first emerged. Repeat as necessary.

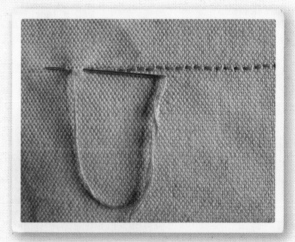

Blanket stitch

This is the classic edging that is seen on lovely old blankets – hence the name. Note how a twisted, rope-like edge is formed at the base of each stitch. Work from left to right.

Bring the needle up at the point where you want the line of stitching to start. Insert it a short distance above and to the right, and bring it out a stitch length below, looping the thread under the needle tip.

Chain stitch

As the name suggests, when worked in a row, this stitch forms a series of loops like a chain. It is often used to embroider trailing stems on flowers. Work from right to left.

Bring the needle up at the point where you want to work the first stitch, then insert it again at the same place. Now bring the needle up a stitch length away, looping the thread under the needle tip, and pull it through. Continue in this way – if you miss the loop, the chain will unravel.

Lazy daisy stitch

This is a variation on chain stitch; in fact, it is also known as detached chain stitch. It is a sweet stitch for sewing daisies onto just about everything – once you get the hang of it, you'll find it's compulsive!

Knot the thread and bring it up from under the fabric. This will become the centre of your daisy. Now insert it again, just to one side of the point it emerged. Bring the needle up a stitch length away, looping the thread under the needle tip, and pull it through. Next take the needle over the thread and make a tiny stitch to catch the looped thread. Bring the needle up in the centre and repeat.

French knot

This makes a sweet little bump and is most used for flower centres.

Bring the needle up through the fabric and wrap the thread two or three times around the needle, keeping the thread pulled taut. Insert the needle just to one side of the point from which it first emerged. You may find that it helps to hold the wrapped thread close to the fabric with the thumbnail of your non-sewing hand as you re-insert the needle.

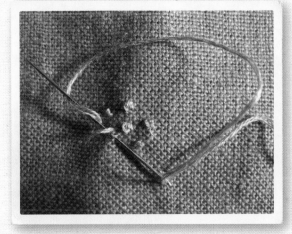

Herringbone stitch

This stitch makes a nice border. Note how the stitches cross over each other at the top and base. Work from left to right.

Bring the needle up at the base of the first stitch. Insert it a short distance above and to the right, and bring it out just to the left of where it went in. Take the needle down in a diagonal line to the baseline again, parallel to the edge and pointing towards the right. Bring it up just to the left of that point. Repeat to get the zig-zag effect.

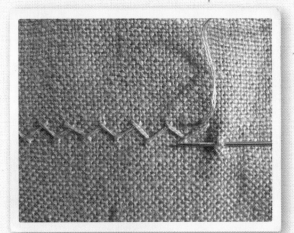

Satin stitch

This is a great stitch for 'filling in' areas such as flower petals.

You may find it helpful to mark out the area that you want to fill, using tailor's chalk or a fadeaway fabric marker pen. Bring the needle up through the fabric at the top of the area and take it down at the bottom. Repeat, leaving no space between your stitches.

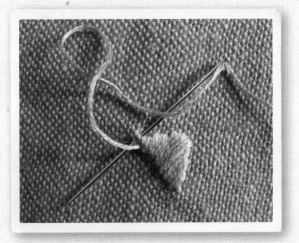

Eyelets

Eyelets are usually brass or chrome and are quite easy to fit once you've worked out which bit goes where. Packs of eyelets include a tool for fitting along with basic instructions. They come in a range of sizes with the size on the pack relating to the hole size rather than the outside of the eyelet. The right side of the eyelet is smooth and the wrong side has ridges.

1 Place the eyelet ring in position and use it as a guide to draw a circle. Mark a cross within the circle and cut along the lines with a craft knife or small sharp scissors. Trim away the inside of the circle leaving a neat round hole just slightly smaller than the middle of the eyelet.

2 Push the raised centrepiece through the hole from the right to the wrong side of the fabric.

3 There is one smooth and one folded edge to the ring part. Slip it over the raised part with the folded edge next to the fabric. Rest the eyelet on the indented ring half of the tool.

4 Place the eyelet tool inside the raised part and grip the handle firmly. Whack the centre of the round end of the tool a few times with a hammer. The centre should now be folded flat onto the ring.

Trimmings

Finishing touches elevate whatever you make by adding individuality, style and colour. If you are going vintage, the trimmings are the key to the look. A thick cotton fringe on a bathroom curtain or pompom braid around a cushion are so very 1950s and contrast piping was big in the '60s and '80s.

Rick-rack

Rick-rack is one of the most enduring and popular braids. It comes in a range of widths from a tiny wiggle to a bold wavy line, with some more rounded or angular than others. It is well worth snapping up any vintage packs, as the colour range was huge in the 1950s. Retro fashion has brought it back into production and it can be bought new online and from most good haberdashery stores.

To sew on rick-rack by hand, bring the needle up from the back of the work and catch a thread at the top and bottom of each curve. If you are using a machine, stitch through the centre of the rick-rack.

Pom-pom braid

Pom-pom braid can be bought in a range of sizes and colours. It's a great way to finish off the bottom of a blind, the edge of a cushion or the lid of a box. For a blind, sew along the top and bottom of the flat tape using a matching thread. For a cushion, hide the tape inside the seam so that only the pom-poms are visible. For a box, either sew the tape to the lid or use strong glue to attach it.

Attach pom-pom braid in the same way as piping cord (see page 151), pinning it around the edge of the cushion front, aligning the tape edge of the braid with the raw edges of the cushion.

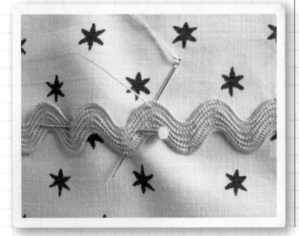

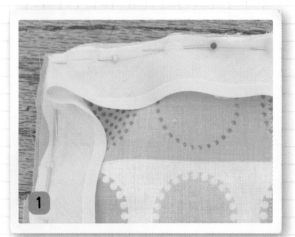

Bias binding

Bias binding can be both functional and decorative. Used on the inside in a matching colour it will finish off a raw edge very neatly. When you use a contrasting colour of binding on the outside, it becomes a design feature. Coloured binding defines the edge and, being cut on the bias, the stretch is across rather than with or against the grain so it works very well on curves and frills.

Binding can be bought ready made or you can make your own.

Attaching bias binding

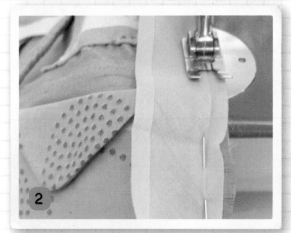

1 Open out the bias binding. With right sides together, aligning the raw edges, pin the binding to the piece being bound. You may wish to tack it in place, too.

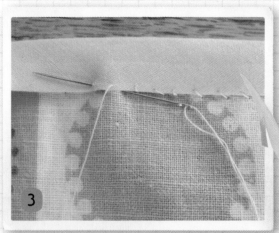

2 Machine stitch along first crease line.

3 Fold the binding over to back of the work, tucking in the raw edge along the crease line, and slipstitch by hand.

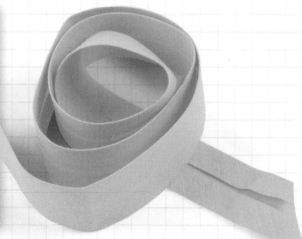

Making your own bias binding

The amount of fabric required to make this is surprisingly economical, but several diagonal strips will have to be joined together to obtain the required length. The strips cut from the middle are the longest and most useful, as they have fewer joins.

1 Fold the fabric diagonally from corner to corner and press the fold. Use a ruler to draw lines 2in (5cm) apart, parallel to the folded edge. Cut along the lines to make fabric strips.

2 Place two strips right sides together, so that the inside edges form a right angle. Sew across at the point where they overlap

3 Fold the binding back along the stitching line and press the seam open. Then fold both long raw edges in and press, and fold the binding in half lengthways and press again.

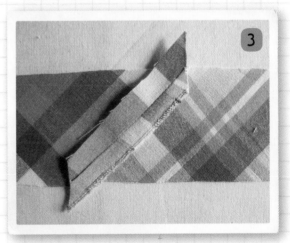

Piping cord

Piping cord gives a really lovely finish to cushions and other projects where you want a defined edge. It can be made in matching or contrasting fabric. You will need a length of bias binding (either ready-made or home-made see pages 148–149) and piping cord, which is available in a range of different widths.

To work out how much piping cord you will need, measure around the edges of the item to which you want to attach it and add an overlap of about 2in (5cm).

Making piping cord

Piping cord can be bought ready made, but it is often hard to find exactly what you're after. The answer is to make your own – it's easy and very satisfying to be in control of the thickness, the colour and pattern.

1 Lay the cord along the centre of the strip of bias binding.

2 Fold over and pin close to the cord, then use a zipper foot to sew a line of stitches right up against the bump of the cord.

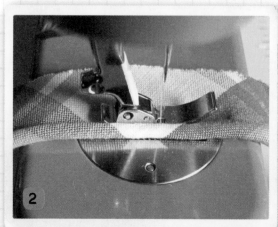

Using cord around a cushion cover

Most of us start out making cushions without piping – but once you've piped, there is no going back! Piping adds structure, definition, contrast and a touch of class.

1 Pin the piping cord around the edge of the cushion front on the right side, making sure that you align the raw edge of the bias binding with the raw edge of the cushion cover. Snip the edge of the fabric up to the stitching when you reach the corners so that the cord turns easily. Sew around the edge, keeping the zipper foot pressed up to the edge of the covered cord. Trim some cord away to flatten the piping where the two ends of the cord meet.

2 Place the back of the cushion on top of the front, right sides together. Sew around the outer edge once again, with the zipper foot pressing up against the piping cord edge. Turn the piped cushion cover the right side out.

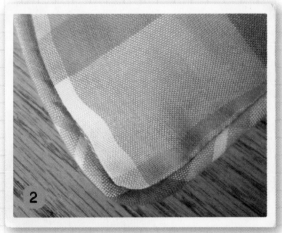

Sewing Terms

Unfamiliar terms can mystify and even discourage some beginners. Although most of the sewing terms that you will encounter are descriptive and self-explanatory, here are a few that are worth learning.

Backstitch In machine sewing, this is the starting and finishing of a seam by reverse stitching over about five stitches, then sewing forwards again. This locks the stitching to prevent it from coming apart.

In hand sewing, a stitch that is both functional (it is the best and sturdiest stitch to join seams by hand) and decorative; see page 143.

Bias The diagonal grain of a fabric, at 45° to the lengthways and crossways grain of the fabric. The most stretch in any fabric is on the diagonal; this is what gives vintage tea dresses their fabulous floaty shape.

Bias binding Narrow, folded strips of fabric cut on the bias; can be home-made (see page 148) or bought ready-made. It is used to cover raw edges and to provide a neat, decorative finish.

Blind hem A hand-sewn hem in which the needle picks up a single thread of the fabric; it is practically invisible on the right side of the work.

Bobbin The small metal or plastic spool that holds the bottom thread in a sewing machine.

Facing Picture a sleeveless dress that is turned inside out: the fabric that surrounds the neck and armholes is called a facing. It is a very neat way of tucking in all the raw edges.

Feed dog Ridged teeth under the needle plate of a sewing machine that move the fabric.

Foot control The start/stop and speed control for a sewing machine.

Fraying The occurence of those annoying wisps of thread that a raw seam edge. When you cut through fabric, the tension in warp threads is relaxed and this is what causes it to fray. Threads of fabric unravel until they meet a line of stitching, more so on a loosely woven fabric. There's a commercially available product called Fray Check, which can be useful if you're doing appliqué and don't want to turn under all those fiddly little edges.

French seam Two pieces are first joined by a seam on the right side of the fabric, then the piece is turned inside out and pressed along the stitching line. A second seam is then sewn on the wrong side of the work, so that the raw edges of the first seam are

tucked inside. A French seam is used to add neatness and strength to an unlined item, such as the Laundry Bag on page 106. It is particularly useful for very fine, sheer fabrics, as the raw edges are completely enclosed and cannot fray.

Grain This describes the direction of the warp and weft threads. Patterns sometimes tell you to cut with or against the grain. 'With the grain' is lengthways; 'against the grain' is crossways.

Hem The turned raw edge, folded and stitched down by hand or machine. A deep hem will add weight and help the fabric hang better.

Interfacing A special fabric used between the outer fabric and lining to stiffen the piece and help it keep its shape. Interfacing is used in collars and cuffs, and to reinforce fine fabrics for buttonholes, and is usually iron-on.

Iron-on/fusible bonding web A tape that melts under the heat of an iron to fuse two fabrics together; also available by the yard (metre), which is useful for appliquéing shapes. It is good for a quick fix hem, but the heat of a tumble drier can have an adverse effect.

Needle plate A removable, flat plate above the bobbin case.

Pressure foot Holds the fabric down and steady while the fabric is being machine stitched.

Raw edge The cut edge before it has been hemmed.

Seam A line of stitching that joins two pieces of fabric together.

Seam allowance The width of fabric between the cut edge and the stitching.

Selvedge (selvage) The densely woven side edge on a roll of fabric that does not fray. It is formed by the returning weft thread, which loops around the warp on the loom.

Tacking (basting) Temporary running stitches worked by hand to hold fabrics together accurately before machine stitching. Use a contrasting colour of thread to make the stitches visible for easy removal.

Topstitch A visible line of stitching on the outside of a piece; it is used to join pieces of fabric and to reinforce an inner seam, as used on jeans.

Wadding (batting) A compressed pad of cotton or polyester backing used to add depth to fabrics. It comes in a variety of depths for quilting and upholstery and is sold by the yard (metre) in several widths. Insulating or heat-reflecting wadding is used in ironing board covers and oven gloves.

Warp The lengthwise threads or yarns of a woven fabric. The warp threads have no stretch in them.

Weft Threads or yarns that run across the width of the fabric, interlacing with the warp yarns. The weft threads will give a little when stretched.

Blogs

Almost paradoxically, the age of the Internet has contributed to the huge revival of interest in hand-made crafts, with enthusiasts the world over keen to share their knowledge and experience. Use it to your advantage and then share your know-how with others!

There are hundreds of sewing blogs out there and, because they are mostly posted by enthusiasts, there is no guarantee that they'll be kept up. Some direct you to their shop, while others generously share their tips and patterns. Some are rich in knowledge and information, while others are divinely personal and quirky.

Run an Internet search for sewing blogs and dip in and out until you locate your personal favourites. Sites such as Folksy and Etsy are online shops for crafters and are also inspiring if you find yourself stuck for ideas.

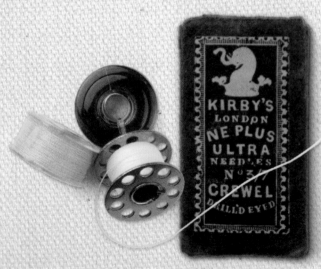

www.burdastyle.com
Burda have been producing dress patterns for decades and they now have a magazine-style blog that is worth a look.

www.freesewingpatternsdaily. blogspot.com
If you have a few hours to spare and feel in a making mood this may be the blog to follow. Jane Blogs really does give you a free pattern with step-by-step instructions every day.

www.hearthandmadeuk.tumblr.com
Inspirational pictures of crafty, hand-made, homey stuff.

www.purlbee.com
A blog from the famous PurlSoho, New York's coolest yarn store. They feature both sewing products and projects too, and it is well worth subscribing to their newsfeed for regular doses of inspiration.

www.thesewingdirectory.co.uk
A great resources directory with news, shopping and crafting information.

www.ukcraftblog.com
A sewing blog directory for the UK.

Suppliers

There used to be one or two specialist shops selling fabrics and haberdashery in every small town, but home sewing went out of fashion and many of them were lost. The good news is that sewing has made a great big comeback!

Although we can now buy almost everything we need online, we all know that there is nothing quite like seeing the true colours and feeling the textures while browsing and dreaming of the possibilities. The even better news is that a new wave of shops are popping up – so keep a look-out in your neighbourhood, because sewing is here to stay.

UK

Calico Laine

Tel: +44 (0)151 3363 939
www.calicolaine.co.uk
This supplier of sewing materials has a good range and reliably fast delivery times. They have shops in Wirral and Cheshire and they also have a telephone sales line manned by very friendly and helpful people.

The Cloth House

47 Berwick Street
London W1F 8SJ
Tel: +44 (0)20 7437 5155
www.clothhouse.com
Stocks an extensive collection of fabrics, from woollens, linens and cottons to fine jerseys and silks. Also supplies by mail order.

The Cotton Patch

1283–1285 Stratford Road
Hall Green
Birmingham B28 9AJ
Tel: +44 (0)121 702 2840
www.cottonpatch.co.uk
Shop and online store specializing in patchwork and quilting fabrics, wadding and haberdashery. If you're looking for print fabrics on a particular theme, this is a great place to start.

Duttons for Buttons

Oxford Street
Harrogate
North Yorkshire HG1 1QE
Tel: +44 (0)1423 502 092
www.duttonsforbuttons.co.uk
All the buttons, zips, trimmings and haberdashery you are ever likely to need! There are two other shops, in Ilkley and York, as well as a reliable mail-order service.

Liberty

Great Marlborough Street
London W1B 5AH
Tel: +44 (0)20 7734 1234
www.liberty.co.uk
This famous London store has always had
a superb sewing department and its Liberty
Lawn fabrics are never out of fashion. It is
incredibly stylish and well worth a visit
just to soak up the atmosphere, although
the temptation to buy is irresistible. Plus an
online shop.

MacCulloch & Wallis

25–26 Dering Street
London W1 S1AT
Tel: +44 (0)20 7629 0311
www.macculloch-wallis.co.uk
The ultimate, old-school haberdashery and
fabric store in central London, plus an online
shop. Frankly, they have it all.

Raystitch

99 Essex Road
London N1 2SL
Tel: +44 (0)20 7704 1060
www.raystitch.co.uk
Be inspired, have a snack, take a course
and buy all you need and more at this
inspirational London haberdashery and café.
You will never want to leave. There is also an
online shop.

Sew Essential

Tel: +44 (0)1922 722276
www.sewessential.co.uk
Online sewing supplies since 2004 with
a massive product range. They are based
in Staffordshire and ship worldwide.

Sewing-online.com

9 Mallard Rd
Victoria Business Park
Netherfield
Nottingham, NG4 2PE
Tel: +44 (0)115 987 4422
www.sewing-online.com
An online haberdashery and supplier
of sewing equipment that is well
worth exploring.

VV Rouleaux

102 Marylebone Lane
London W1U 2QD
Tel: +44 (0)207 224 5179
www.vvrouleaux.com
An inspirational source of ribbons and
all kinds of trimmings to give your projects
that all-important finishing touch.

A must read:

SELVEDGE magazine is all about creativity
and textiles. It is always beautiful to look
at and crammed with interesting features.
Ask for a subscription as a gift and you
will be hooked.
www.selvedge.co.uk

USA

Craft and Fabric Links
www.craftandfabriclinks.com
Suppliers for crafty and general
sewing projects.

Michael Miller Fabrics
118 West 22nd Street
5th Floor
New York, NY 10011
Tel: +1 212 704 0774
www.michaelmillerfabrics.com
A fabulous source of retro and contemporary
fabrics. Available online and from various
retailers, details of which can be found on
the website.

Sew, Mama, Sew!
PO Box 1127
Beaverton
Oregon, 97075
Tel: +1 503 380 3584
www.sewmamasew.com
Vast choice of fabric and an inspirational,
easy-to-navigate website.

Acknowledgements

Author's acknowledgments

I would like to thank Stewart and Rupert for their
patience, and promise that I will now clear the kitchen
table of all sewing paraphernalia.

My most useful reference books on sewing are a
battered copy of *The Batsford Book of Sewing* by Ann
Ladbury (published 1967) and *The Reader's Digest
Complete Guide to Needlework* (published 1983).

Publisher's acknowledgments

Step photography by Sally Walton. Other photography
by Tim Clinch and Gilda Pacitti. Picture research by
Hedda Roennevig.

With thanks to the following for their help with props,
assistance and locations for the photography in this
book: A & Y Cumming Ltd., Lewes, Virginia Brehaut,
Emma Foster, Emma Kennedy, Jenny Statham and
Harry, Rhoda Barker and Christian Funnell at The
Old Forge in South Heighton.

Liberty Art Fabrics Tana Lawn available from www.
liberty.co.uk: page 1 Carline; pages 36–39 Capel;
pages 58–61 Poppy & Honesty; pages 66–69 Fairford;
pages 74–77 Wiltshire; pages 78–83 Capel R: pages
88–91 Wiltshire; pages 96–99 Capel; pages 106–109
Wiltshire; pages 110–113 Dora.

Index

A

aprons 18, 19, 66–69, 70–73
artist's canvas 46

B

backstitch 143, 152
basting *see* tacking
Bath Cap 28, 110–113
batting *see* wadding
bias 152
bias bindings 148–149, 152
biodegradability of natural
    fabrics 120
blanket stitch 143
blind hems 152
blogs 154
bobbins 152
bodkins 125
bonding web, fusible
    125, 131, 153
bound hems 132
boxes, storage 13, 44–47
Butcher's Apron 19, 70–73
buttonholes 139, 140
buttons 138

C

chain stitch 144
coat hangers 23, 91
Coffee Cozy 16, 58–61
colour fastness 120, 121
cotton wadding 50, 58, 92
cushions 10, 32–35, 151
cutting methods
    126, 127, 140

D

Doorstop 11, 36–39

E

elastic, stitching of 113
embroidery stitches 143–145
Envelope Cushion 10, 32–35
Eye Mask 24, 92–95
eyelets 106, 146

F

fabric predictability 120, 126
fabrics, sourcing
    80, 84, 88, 120–121
facings 152
fastenings 138–142
feed dogs 152
finishing seams 133–135
foot control 152
fraying 152
french knots 145
french seams 152–153
fusible bonding web
    125, 131, 153

G

gathering 136–137
glossary 152–153
grain 153

H

Hairstyling Bag 29, 114–117
hand sewing *see also* stitches
    backstitch 152
    buttonholes 140

buttons 138
gathering 136
hemming 130, 131, 132
heat-reflecting wadding
    50, 58, 153
hemming 130–132, 152, 153
hemming stitch 131
herringbone stitch 132, 145
hook-and-loop tapes 141
hooks and eyes 142

I

information sources
    125, 154–155
interfacing 153
interlining 92, 94
iron-on bonding web
    125, 131, 153
ironing 125, 135
Ironing Board Cover
    15, 54–57

J

Jewellery Roll 25, 96–99

L

lace, fitting 82
Laundry Bag 27, 106–109
lazy daisy stitch 144

M

machine sewing
    72, 87, 122, 128–129
machine stitching
    backstitch 152

buttonholes 139
gathering 137
hemming 130, 132
over pins 35, 130
measuring fabric 40
mount boards 46

N

natural fabrics 120
needle threaders 125
needles 72, 87, 122, 123
Nightdress or Pyjama Case
    21, 80–83

O

'on the fold' cutting 127
Oven Gloves 14, 50–53
oversewn seam allowances
    135

P

Padded Coat Hanger
    23, 88–91
patterns 126–127
Peg Bag 17, 62–65
pinked seam allowances 134
pinking shears 124, 134
pinning 130
pins 123
piping cord 150–151
Plastic Bag Keeper 20, 74–77
polyester wadding 50, 54, 92
pom-pom braid 147
poppers 142
press studs 142
pressing 135
pressure foot 153
Pretty Girly Apron 18, 66–69
pyjama cases 21, 80–83

Q

quilter's wadding 58, 92

R

raw edges 153
recyling
    fabrics
        80, 84, 88, 120, 121
    sewing threads 121
    wadding 56
retro-style fabrics 121
rick-rack 147

S

safety pins 125
satin stitch 145
scissors 124
Screen Cover 12, 40–43
seam allowances
    133, 134–135, 153
seam rippers 124
seams 133–135, 152–153
selvedge (selvage) 153
sewing blogs 154
sewing kits 122–125
sewing machines
    87, 122, 152
sewing supplies 155–156
sewing terminology 152–153
shoe bags 22, 84–87
silk 87
stitches
    backstitch 143, 152
    blanket 143
    chain 144
    french knots 145
    hemming 131
    herringbone 132, 145
    lazy daisy 144

satin 145
topstitch 153
Storage Box 13, 44–47
suppliers 155–156

T

tacking 130, 153
tailor's chalk 124
tape measures 124
thimbles 124
threads 121, 125, 137
topstitch 153
tracing patterns 126
Travel Shoebag 22, 84–87
trimming seam allowances
    133–134
trimmings 147–151

U

unpickers 124

V

vintage fabrics 120

W

wadding
    50, 54, 56, 58, 90, 92, 153
warp 153
Wash Bag 26, 102–105
washing fabrics 126
waterproof fabrics 102, 111
weft 153

Z

zig-zagged seam allowances
    134
zips 104, 141

To place an order, or to
request a catalogue, contact:

GMC Publications, Castle Place,
166 High Street, Lewes,
East Sussex, BN7 1XU
United Kingdom

Tel: +44 (0)1273 488005
Fax: +44 (0)1273 402866

www.gmcbooks.com